Nauset Light:

A Personal Legacy

Mary E. Daubenspeck
Timothy H. Daubenspeck

Keeper's House Press

Published 2024 by Keeper's House Press
Colchester, VT
www.nausetlightkeepershouse.com

Paperback ISBN: 979-8-218-41643-0
Ebook ISBN: 979-8-218-41644-7
Library of Congress Control Number: 2024909273

Images from the Daubenspeck collection
Cover design and interior design by librodesign.com

Time and tide wait for no man...

— Geoffrey Chaucer

Contents

This work is dedicated to Miriam L. Rowell and her husband Lucien, to Mary Daubenspeck, and the Daubenspeck Family of Brothers, their families, and their close circle of friends with whom they collectively maintained and preserved the Keeper's House for the 23 years following Mary's death and prior to expiration of their Special Use Permit in 2024. Also, to the Nauset Light Preservation Society (NLPS) and the Cape Cod National Seashore (CCNS), without whose support a complete Nauset Light Station would not exist. And finally, to my dear Paula who has lent a shine both to the Keeper's House and to my life and, in so doing, has helped to make this endeavor possible.

—Tim Daubenspeck

Preface

This book is largely based on the lively and spontaneous real-time journaling of Mary Daubenspeck, the private owner of the Nauset Light Keeper's House, as she grappled with the forces of nature and mankind to secure a safe destiny for the Nauset Light Keeper's House and Oil House during the erosion crisis that threatened the Nauset Light Station in the 1990s.

During her lifetime, Mary was an accomplished writer with a gift for articulating her thoughts and impressions of events in a manner that revealed a deep humanity and an endearing self-awareness. Her life was remarkably full and complex, and she was blessed with an extraordinary "can-do" energy level, a fine intellect, and a wonderful sense of humor.

At the time of her death from cancer in 2001, at the age of 56, Mary had only recently managed to ensure the long-term integrity of the Nauset Light Station through a partnership agreement with the Cape Cod National Seashore (CCNS). She did so by selflessly donating both the Keeper's House and the Oil House in exchange for their relocation to safety on public land and a 25-year permit (for Mary and family) to continue to use the Keeper's House as a private dwelling.

Mary's association with the Nauset Light Keeper's House began with her private purchase of it in 1982 (with her husband), the early years of her ownership having been described in her first book, *Nauset Light: A Personal History,* published in 1995.[2] Her intention had been to publish a second book in which she would complete her "personal history" as it played out with the restoration of the tripartite Light Station, but fate did not afford her this opportunity.

Now, in 2024, as the Daubenspeck private occupancy term expires and operational responsibilities for the Keeper's House are being turned over to CCNS and the Nauset Light Preservation Society (NLPS),[3] it is time for the rest of Mary's intended story to be told. While it is my great privilege to attempt this, I could never have hoped on my own to relate it as well as Mary could have. But I am fortunate that I don't really have to — because Mary's journals enable the story to be told largely in her own voice, with minimal supporting narrative necessary to maintain the reader's perspective.

I write this at what is an incomprehensibly sad personal moment for my family and me. We are a close-knit group, and as the only sister among five brothers, Mary has always held a prominent place in each of our hearts. She indeed "leavened" our lives with her generous loving and caring nature and her wonderful sense of humor.

Mary's Keeper's House and the Nauset Lighthouse have been a family focal point for more than 40 years, and as we now relinquish responsibility for the house and hand over the keys, we are overcome with a profound sense of loss. Having had more than two decades to anticipate this moment has not made it any less difficult. Our families and our children have grown up with the annual summer vacations and reunions at the Keeper's House, and over the past few years, the new and emergent generation of nieces, nephews, and grandchildren has begun to build lifelong memories there.

The deeper significance of this transition is clearly about "loss" — a life theme with multiple facets and embodiments, but in this case, as much about our family's loss of Mary herself as about anything else. With Nauset the symbol, we all feel a tangible, if illusory, piece of Mary slipping away that we have somehow held on to for many years by having preserved and maintained her Keeper's House in the manner she had originally inspired.

Mary's passion for the Keeper's House and the Nauset Light Station and her overriding sense of personal responsibility have proven to be the dynamic effectual forces behind the long-term preservation of the three landmark structures together — Lighthouse, Keeper's House, and Oil House — in their now permanent, historic, proximal orientation. Mary's lived experience of the years just before, during, and after the Lighthouse relocation (1996) and Keeper's House move (1998) were fraught with stress and anxiety as she fought the good fight. She was a stalwart lone advocate for the Keeper's House, determined to make the "right" things happen in the face of limited options while metered by Nature's clock in the form of the advancing front of the Atlantic against the Eastern Cape Cod shore.

This is the story in Mary's own words — of her life during that time, that struggle, and ultimately its hard-won outcome for the greater good. Mary's personal eyewitness account of the Lighthouse relocation makes for delightful reading and brings the human dimension of that historic event to life. Her spirit lives on in the experience of her family and friends who've lived out the term of her Special Use Permit, and in her public legacy to the Cape Cod community, with the Keeper's House and Oil House permanently affixed in their historic positions together with Nauset Light.

View of Light through trellised patio at previous Keeper's House location circa 1990.

Nauset Light Station from south ca. 1985 (prior to 1996/1998 relocations).

Nauset Light Station from west ca. 2015 (after 1996/1998 relocations).

Introduction

The Nauset Light Keeper's House in Eastham, Massachusetts, was built in 1875 by the United States government and situated immediately adjacent to the Three Sisters Lighthouses for the purpose of providing a residence for the lightkeeper and his family. Since construction, it has stood proudly behind the Light, withstanding the unrelenting tests of time, weather, and mankind, to this very moment (2024) as it makes its final transition from private management to a lasting future securely linked to Nauset Light in the public domain. Now in its second location, having been rescued once previously from a watery demise in 1923, the relative position and orientation of the Keeper's House with respect to the Lighthouse has been retained for historical authenticity.

This work serves as a sequel to the original book[1] by Mary Daubenspeck (vanRoden) entitled *Nauset Light: A Personal History*, published in 1995, which described Mary's private purchase of the Keeper's House from her forebear, Miriam Rowell, in 1982. Miriam and her husband, Col. Lucien A. Rowell, were the first "live-in" private owners of the Keeper's House, having bought it in 1957 from the Boston judge William Shaw McCallum.[3]

As described in Mary's book, she and Miriam Rowell were "cut from the same cloth" and both shared a common sense of personal responsibility to the historic preservation of the Keeper's House that exceeded their own desires for personal gain. For Miriam's part, in 1982 she had the opportunity to sell the house to several interested, wealthy prospective buyers. Miriam selected Mary in recognition of an immediate mutual sense of "kindred," the two having become fast friends in their initial meetings. Miriam and Mary quickly discovered in one another a similar perspective on life that included a remarkable appreciation for — and a deep devotion to — preservation and posterity, specifically with respect to the ultimate importance of the Keeper's House as an integral part of the Nauset Light Station. For Mary's part, the rapidly accelerating dune barrier erosion rate during her tenure of ownership forced her into the position of having to make the tough calls on behalf of the Keeper's House, amidst a dynamic of adversity.

This firsthand account of Mary's personal commitment to the Keeper's House, the relocation of the Nauset Light Station, and her decision to gift the Keeper's House to the Cape Cod National Seashore (CCNS) is also the modern story of the life of the Keeper's House. While the landmark structures (Lighthouse, Keeper's House, and Oil House) were never physically separated from one another (other than briefly during the relocation process) during Mary's private ownership, they very nearly became split permanently. Had it not been for Mary's overriding sense of a greater obligation, they most assuredly would have been.

The Nauset Lighthouse, Keeper's House, and Oil House together comprise what is indisputably one of the most iconic and visually impressive landmarks in New England. The familiar trio serves as the identifying emblem for the Town of Eastham, the Cape Cod Potato Chips company (logo), and even the Cape itself — as evidenced by the local vehicle license plate design and the "Welcome to Cape Cod" signs on the highway approaches to the Bourne and Sagamore bridges.

As the owner of two of the three imperiled structures, and point person in determining their ultimate destiny, Mary poured her heart and soul into supporting the historical site's integrity while trying desperately to balance that public interest against her own looming financial loss. With urgency — against diminishing time in the face of the punishing advance of the Atlantic Ocean — she fought to elevate the Keeper's House relocation project to the "radar" of the landowning Cape Cod National Seashore (CCNS), with the irony that, in doing so, she helped to set in motion a process that would bring with it a very dear personal cost.

Mary Daubenspeck circa 1995.

Mary struggled mightily with the tensions associated with her perceived mission. On the one hand lay the practical and financially compelling considerations that augured towards moving the House to a private site away from the Lighthouse. In the absence of a reasonable alternative this is perhaps what most of us might have done, thinking to preserve investment and family access. However, the nobler part of Mary's spirit labored with her visceral grasp of the mutual interdependence of the two critical structures and their consequent synergy of identity — knowing well that neither without the other held the impactful symbolic power of the two of them together.

Temporary separation of Lighthouse and Keeper's House between relocation of Lighthouse (November 1996) and Keeper's House (October 1998), captures only a hint at what might have become permanent.

As Mary wrote in her book,[1] "A tower without a setting; a setting without a tower — neither should be the fate of the Nauset Light Station. Because what draws people to the Nauset Light Station — to photograph it, to paint it, to appreciate it — is not just the Lighthouse itself. It is (to use architect Conrad Nobili's elegant phrase) the "proud composition" of all three historic structures, standing together atop this cliff."

As her relationship with the preservation-minded but impassive controlling power of CCNS became somewhat adversarial at times, Mary struggled at length in pursuit of her two main goals — the sustainability of a tripartite Nauset Light Station AND of her private ownership of the Keeper's House — without the benefit of knowing that against the operative backdrop these two objectives were, in fact, mutually incompatible. And, when once it became clear to her that they were indeed in direct competition with one another, Mary acted according to the one she believed to be morally most appropriate, to her own financial detriment.

To the casual onlooker, none of this behind-the-scenes turmoil was evident. Had the final outcome involved the unthinkable — and permanent — disassociation of these structures, however, it would have surely triggered a profoundly enduring sense of regional disappointment, if not a virtual crisis of local identity.

Perhaps the most engaging aspect of this tale is that it is told mostly from Mary's perspective and in her own words, from her real-time journaling and Keeper's Log writing. Now, twenty-three years after her death, her wonderful, reflective independent record-keeping breathes vibrant life into this story for the benefit of any or all who may have an interest — whether it be historical, communal, literary, or personal.

At this point in 2024, as Keeper's House management responsibility transitions back to within the auspices of the Park Service, documentation for the record is both warranted and timely — but the story of Mary's altruism will live for as long as the Nauset Light landmark remains one of the most beautiful and treasured visitation sites on Cape Cod. This, then, is the record that should never be lost and the purpose of telling this story.

Mary's Keeper's House Prior to 1995

Background

Mary describes some of her early Keeper's House ownership years in her book chapter entitled "On My Watch."[1] She recounts how she came to be the owner in early 1982, after being chosen from a group of wealthy prospective buyers by Miriam Rowell for her particular suitability. From Miriam's viewpoint, Mary clearly and deeply understood that the personal value of the house as a premium asset for personal enjoyment and investment was eclipsed by its regional significance as an identifying and historic outer-Cape treasure, ultimately intended for all to enjoy in posterity.

Mary's experience growing up as the only daughter in a close-knit family of six children in coastal suburban southern Connecticut prepared her well for the world (having survived home life with five brothers) and imbued in her a remarkable ability to accept its challenges with a positive "can-do" attitude. As a young woman, she successfully completed the Hurricane Island Outward Bound School's first all-women's 26-day sea sailing course in Maine, which included a three-day solo survival stint on an island in Penobscot Bay.

Mary Daubenspeck – 1974 photo at Hurricane Island.

An English major graduate of Bryn Mawr college, she had a natural inclination towards language and communications and an innate facility with words that enabled her to articulate her views with candor, color, and humor. Thus, her journal writings yield a glimpse into her perspective on many aspects of her multifaceted life, but particularly on her Keeper's House ownership and its (and her) erosion dilemma during the last 19 years of her life. To that end, selections from her journals are culled out posthumously for the benefit of relating this important part of her personal story intertwined with the life of the Keeper's House.

As principal narrator and co-author of this sequel, I am Mary's younger brother by 10 years, the fourth in the sibling line of six. Mary had a very close relationship with each of her five brothers, but because she and I found ourselves both somewhat unexpectedly experiencing mid-life as single people (again) in the 1990s, we were able to spend time doing things together. I occasionally had the good fortune to accompany her to the Keeper's House during the years of planning and decision-making leading up to the relocation of the House in 1998.

Having been able to attend some of the determinative meetings that were held in CCNS conference rooms in 1995–1996 to discuss the fate of the Keeper's House, I developed a sense of the operative dynamics affecting this matter. Later then, in 2001, as she faced Stage 4 colon cancer and was ordering her personal affairs, she asked me to take over the reins as the primary point person for management of the Keeper's House through the term of the Special Use Permit, to 2024. She passed away in New Hampshire in March of 2001. Subsequently, and with a good deal of assistance from my elder brother Andy, I was privileged to have been able to oblige and honor her wish.

Mary's Private Ownership Prior to Erosion Crisis (1981–1989)

At the time of purchasing the Keeper's House, in the winter of 1982, Mary had been dealing with some significant life challenges, including ulcerative colitis and a difficult marital situation. The writer and poet within, struggling to make sense of life, its purpose and its impermanence, was awakened to a lengthy period of introspection and spiritual curiosity, and through that, a reinvigoration of her Christian faith.

Her personal appreciation of the unlikely set of coincidences that had enabled her meeting Miriam Rowell and coming into private ownership of the Keeper's House (described in her first book[1]) left her with a feeling that her life path had turned a phase anew and that a window of spirit and soul had been opened.

What for Mary had perhaps begun as a romantic flight of fancy had somewhat suddenly become a solid reality as the object of her fascination came squarely into view, per Miriam's marked preference to sell the house only to her. And so was born a personal mission, metaphoric in its resonance with Mary's own spiritual orientation.

Her extraordinarily quick and deep bond with Miriam was rooted, in part, in their shared existential awareness of their individual capability and simultaneous fragility that Miriam stoically modeled as she faced myriad age-related health issues. The tenacity of Miriam's spirit won Mary's admiration and respect, as she likely saw in Miriam a good bit of herself. And through both of their human lives ran the parallel theme embodied by the Lighthouse and Keeper's House — of strength, courage, and grace in the face of daunting adversity.

As Miriam rested on her deathbed in Boston in early April 1983, Mary wrote:

Miriam is dying. She is now hospitalized for a brain inflammation resulting from her cancer spreading to her brain. She is losing her battle with the cancer that only <u>she</u> *knew had begun in her lungs. Cae Barton says that she probably only has a few days left. The box of Lighthouse history raw materials lies in my basement waiting for me to take it up to her so she can go through it with me, so I can write Draft #1 of the history. I had just mailed a note to her asking if I could put off our dinner date from April 18th until the 25th so I could go to a board meeting I'd forgotten about, and a theater board mini retreat... Nope. It's already too late. I will never again see my old friend Miriam over a nice dinner with lots of laughter and long stories about her wonderfully active life and eternally aggressive spirit. I close my eyes to pray for her and the words that come are, "Thy will be done."*

Miriam Rowell happened into my life and occupied a space she must have been destined for — it's like I have always known her, and it has been that way ever since I first spoke to her on the telephone, November 3, 1981. I love Miriam Rowell, and I have since I met her. I want to see her and recapture once again that great indomitable spirit that is hers, and now I know I can't do that. I am losing something in a way, but even now as I write this, the word "losing" asks to be changed: I am LETTING GO of Miriam, not losing her.

I am willing to let go of her probably because I know I <u>won't</u> lose her. The Lighthouse Keeper's cottage will continue to hold her; her garden will; that cliff will; every one of those birds she left behind up there will. And so will every indelible memory of our brief path-crossing. Oh, Miriam. Go gently, if you must go.

Miriam died on April 13, 1983. Mary flew up to Providence from her then-primary home outside Philadelphia and drove out to Eastham in a rental car for the funeral. Through mutual friends, Mary had offered the Keeper's House as the venue for Miriam's funeral service, which took place on Saturday April 16th. She described it in her journal entry dated **"April 16–17 in Eastham"**:

I'd forgotten my keys, so I went right to Cae's where we sat down to a nice lunch that Cae had thoughtfully prepared — cheese soufflé, a strawberry and yogurt Bibb lettuce salad, and coffee — and as always happens at that table, we talked as if we'd all known each other all our lives. Good people like Cae and Chas attract and keep good people around them, and they share them unstintingly with others like me who are each time amazed at how quickly strangers can become fast friends in an atmosphere of love and trust.

I left and went to the cottage to see what needed doing, while the others (except Chas) made ready to come to the funeral service. The place was set with about 50 old wooden folding chairs with dome-shaped bent wood backs, those in the sitting room and kitchen facing the north and those in the parlor facing west. The minister from the Church of the Holy Spirit in Orleans (Episcopal, via Cae) was to stand at the north window in the kitchen, between the toaster oven and the coffee maker, right near Miriam's anchor, that big commercial gas range with the enormous hood. Miriam wasn't connected with a church. I wonder if she secretly came to faith before she died.

On each chair seat was a pamphlet printed up by the funeral director (Nickerson). Flowers sent by half a dozen people were placed around, and there were three beauteous, pink, large-flowered azalea bushes about the kitchen, which Cae had bought for a triangle-memorial for Miriam: one on the grave, one in Cae's yard, and one at the Lighthouse Keeper's cottage. The place never looked nicer — it did indeed look very much the way Miriam had always had it, and as the 60 or so people who came began to arrive, nearly all remarked about that. All also said how nice it was of me to lend the place for this occasion, to which I could only reply that I have always thought of it as Miriam's place; I have been taking care of it for her while she's been away. I wondered to myself as I said this if now the place would begin to feel like mine. I wasn't sure I wanted it to feel any different...

The next morning, I hopped out of bed, looked out the window, said "Good Morning Miriam!", and went over to the seaward window to see what the ocean looked like. As I stood there for several minutes, I noted that it felt somehow different today than it had on every other day when I've stood looking out that window. This morning I felt a strange tinge of loneliness, a feeling of being alone on a point where a short time ago others had stood too. It struck me that Miriam's house had now become my house, Miriam's view out this window was now my view out this window. Miriam was not "just away," Miriam was now gone forever. And yet her memory hovered all about me. It was a strange shift in perception which I can't adequately put into words.

And a little later that year during personal time at the Keeper's House, an excerpt from a letter by Mary to a dear friend:

I am in my own compromised way doing little bits of a similar thing this year, coming out here to the place we bought in January of 1982 for rest, relaxation and — now that most of the real work is done to make the place really nice again — rediscovery. Self-rediscovery, yes, but also rediscovery of the natural forces which are so evident out here on this oversized sandbar where my parents brought us for 12 consecutive summer vacations. I hadn't been back here for 13 years when I had the truly incredible good fortune of becoming aware of and being able to buy a one of a kind retreat here, one which is steeped in history and faces an uncertain future, and because of all that, serves as an island in time (my time, geologic time, historical time). Something to crawl up on in the stream of events (my events, geologic events, world events), then take some deep renewing breaths on, before diving back into "the real (?) world" of un-refused obligations.

The house was built in 1875 as the lighthouse keeper's dwelling for the "Three Sisters of Nauset" (for more on these first early Nauset Lights, see "Part One: The Early Years" in Mary's first book[3]), three lighthouses all in a row on this cliff, warning vessels en route to and from Boston (pre-Cape Cod Canal) of the nasty shoals just offshore which have claimed an astounding number of vessels, cargoes, and lives over the last 350 years. The house has been moved back from the advancing erosion once already (1923) and will within my anticipated lifetime need another move, as the cliff is losing two feet per year on the average and the house sits about 35– 40 years from the edge now.

Aftermath of February nor'easter and power loss with Light out.

The property, entirely within the protection of the Cape Cod National Seashore, comprises about four acres including 429 feet of Ocean Beach, which is an unbelievable thing to own, as well as an invaluable treasure trove of beauty and discovery. When, several times a day, I go out and stand atop the cliff and look out to sea, I am always astounded when I look to the left (north) and as far as the (even binocular-ed) eye can see, there is unspoiled — yea, even unused — beach stretching into the distance. This summer yet, I am going to pack a day pack and set out at dawn to see if I can't walk all the way to Provincetown on that beach, a distance I estimate to be about 25 miles.

The house, and the 48-foot lighthouse, just off the front porch, are things of awesome beauty in all weather, but especially in winter during horizontal snowstorms which pack the north side of the Light in crystalline snow and ice, creating a small glacier which later slides ever so slowly down the tower and onto the steps like frozen icing off a tipsy cake. And the sunrises popping out of the ocean... and the clearest of skies with hundreds of stars prickling out of it... this is truly a refuge for me, and I wonder what I did to deserve such an option... You must come and see it sometime!

After her purchase of the Keeper's House, Mary graciously began to encourage each of her close relatives and friends, especially her brothers and their families, to make plans to spend time — either with her or independently — at this, her seaside jewel. Among the earliest invitees, I first visited the Keeper's House in June 1982. My wife and I drove up from UCONN after picking up Mary's husband, Don, a pharmaceutical company executive who'd been in Hartford on business. We arrived together at the Keeper's House only to realize that not one of us had a key — particularly problematic since Mary was not due to meet us there until the next day. I remember discovering the small window on the porch to be inadequately locked, and as a relatively nimble 27-year-old, I was able to contort my 6-foot frame in such a way as to get my head and shoulders into the opening. With the aid of some "Pooh"-like pushing from my travel companions, I managed to writhe my way through to the staircase on the other side. After we had opened things up and settled in a bit, we headed out to what was then the Eastham Lobster Pool, a vibrant and traditionally well-packed area favorite, for their infamous lobster and clam dinner.

For me, this visit was a much welcomed and long-in-coming recon-nection with traditional summer family Cape time, having had the privilege of vacationing on the Cape as a kid each year in the 1960s. During our annual rental of a summer cottage in Truro, the Cape had managed to permanently infuse itself in my blood. I had ventured back as a wayward late adolescent a few times with friends, sleeping on the beach, in random dunes, at rest areas in the back of my pickup truck, or in seemingly remote stretches of woods — never with a real place to *stay* but always with a real sense of place to *be*. My own life had since taken on a sober dimension of purpose and direction, and now, as a more disciplined, educated, and married young man, the ordered parallelism of a new and legitimate connection to the Cape was not lost on me.

Most of this story is based on the writings of Mary Daubenspeck, as entered into her personal journal in real time during her tenure as owner of the Nauset Lightkeeper's House.

Other material comes from the guest logbook, maintained over the years in the Keeper's House, into which Mary and nearly every visitor recorded some brief insight, observation, or token remembrance upon departure after their stay. These entries are being preserved as a treasured Daubenspeck family record, spanning 42 years from 1982 to 2024. Dated entries are extracted from Mary's personal journal unless otherwise designated as being from the "Keeper's Log" (Keep-er's House guest book). Italics are used (with few exceptions) to distinguish Mary's writing voice from the writing of others and my own contributions. Mary's personal journal entries extend to about 2000, after which the remaining notes are from visitors and the Keeper's Log.

Keeper's Log with sample page from Mary's journal and original Turkish macrame Keeper's House key fob given to Mary by Miriam in 1982.

Winding dune path near Keeper's House beneath white clouds.

Without further ado —

Notes from a Modern Keeper's Life

In early **October 1983**, Mary writes:

At times I am overwhelmed by the appropriateness of things I find cast into my path. For example, today as I sit in my big brass bed, with the sound of the Atlantic Ocean and an early autumn breeze blending with a late summer sunrise, pouring into my bedroom and warming me even through my covers, I picked up my "Diary of Private Prayer"[5] and read:

"O Light that never fades, as the light of day now streams through these windows and floods this room, so let me open to Thee the windows of my heart, that all my life may be filled by the radiance of Thy presence. Let no corner of my being be unillumined by the light of Thy countenance. Let there be nothing within me to darken the brightness of the day. Let the spirit of Him whose life was the light of men rule within my heart till eventide. Amen."

Outside the ocean glistens and shimmers like a thin metal skin about to melt away in the light; the spartina grass and wax-leafed shrubs on the cliff shine like dots and dashes of light in a dark green ground. Earlier this summer, the feeling out on the patio at midday in the sunlight, surrounded by the olive trees and the frequent bird-visitors, made me think of the striking and unsuspected similarity between this place and "Bois Neuf," our occasional mountaintop spring retreat in Saint Barthelemy. So similar was it, that I thought this place might aptly be named "Bois North." Today that feeling is even more justified: there is this similarity of being high up on a ledge overlooking — indeed looking down on — the ocean, the unbelievable absence of any but natural sounds, the feeling that everything I can see and hear from here is of an uninterrupted wholeness, needing not a bit of editing to be perfect, personally and therapeutically supportive. I can feel my colitis remitting!

Mary's philosophical inclinations were deeply introspective and intellectual, leading her at times to experience intensities of spiritual conflict, conflict that she was often uniquely able to put into words, and which the peace and solitude of the Keeper's House enabled her to capture and confront. The magnificent natural setting does tend to awaken the spiritual dimension, heightening self-awareness and activating a potential for personal growth. At the same time affording respite for the soul and body, both so sorely needed then — and she began to realize that she was indeed already beginning to find it there.

Further along in the same journal entry:

It is well past 9:00 in the morning and I'm still sitting here in bed with my books and crossword puzzles and diary and dogs; out the window the ocean still rushes and glitters, the birds are gone or quiet, and a breeze has come up, whisking now and then right through the room. I've talked on the telephone to Mom and Dad and Tim and Steve, explaining why I won't be anywhere but right here for the next three days at least. And it all seems so wonderfully unplanned and self-indulgent, and RIGHT for a change. Every now and then I imagine how it would be if anyone else — anyone — were also here with me on this trip, and I am sad to say that if anyone else were, this would be a very different experience. I would be out of bed and into an empty day trying to fill it with mutually acceptable plans-for-plan's-sake. I'd be thinking about what to make for dinner. I'd be inventing errands and making lists and taking the dogs to the beach. In other words, I'd be making my mission to minister unto others' wants and needs; no way I would be sitting around in bed doing what it seems I really want to do for myself. Even that seems somehow reprehensible: that what I do when left alone must be what I really want to do, and in this case that is exactly nothing. Or is it? Is writing nothing? Is resting nothing? Is getting better after three years of illness nothing? If I think so when others are around doesn't that mean I don't believe myself? That I think more about what others <u>might</u> think than I think about what I think? Whose life is this anyway? Whose health is this? And why is it that the mind creates conflict *in peace and wishes desperately for peace in the conflict that's created? I'm delighted to be alone here now — this is a real island in time I've climbed up on and I'm not going to leave it for a while yet. And, yes, I am grateful for such self-indulgent opportunities. Thank you one and all who made them possible. And now I think I'll read...*

and what I read is this:

"Find out how much God has given you and from it take what you need; the remainder which you do not require is needed by others, the superfluities of the rich are the necessities of the poor. Those who retain what is superfluous possess the goods of others." —Saint Augustine

Later in October, a Monday:

Returning from a "Dutch dinner" at Cae's, I went out to the edge of the cliff to check the surf. Again, tonight it is big. It has been high since Sunday. Each time I go to the edge in daylight I see clumps of wildflowers caught in their descent to the sea, evidencing no concern for what used to be (safety atop the cliff), nor for what is soon to be (dissolution in the stormy surf); instead they cling for as long as they can to what they have left — maybe as little as a handful of soil — and show their lavender and yellow colors while half their roots wave in the breeze as the soil beneath them is cut away by wind and rain and, indirectly, waves. Tonight, as the waves crashed and rolled below and the easterly wind blew fine sand like a sharp mist, I could almost imagine how those tiny flowers feel. I wonder how long it will be before our cottage's roots wave in those winds, and where I'll put the house for its third life.

It wasn't long after Mary's acquisition of the Keeper's House that she became acutely aware of its dynamic status in the face of the threat of the implacable forces of nature and climate.

Wednesday, October 12, 1983: *Outside, there rages a sou'easter with steady 20–30 mile per hour winds and rain that comes and goes — or so it sounds; I've been too cozy in my winterized cottage to go out and do more than listen to the bashing surf from the porch. That same surf, which has* *been 4–6 feet all week, has done interesting things to the beach: like a crazed exterior decorator, it installs a ledge of sand like a miniature cliff for as far as the eye can see, about knee-high, a nice dry perch to watch the waves break from only 10–15 feet out, foaming up to the mini-cliff, then being stopped abruptly by it before they douse one's shoes. Next tide cuts away at it making it sharper of edge. The third high tide breaks into the cliff a way up the beach, and the penetrating sea slush makes a lagoon near the foot of the cliff, which is about the size of a small backyard. Finally, the next tide comes and goes in the night, and when I check the beach from my cliff the next morning, the little graven image of what I stand on has disappeared.*

"Bench" formation in beach sand during erosion process.

Reduction of "bench" and slow motion sand cascade during erosion process. Sand from dune backfills beach sand loss over time, replicating the process.

The beach is now its usual flat sloping self again, its novel construction shaved off and carried elsewhere, southwards down the beach probably. This afternoon, all kinds of thoughts about erosion-control cropped up in my head as I did mindless fix-it tasks like replacing a windowpane in the storm door, rewiring the wind speed indicator, and putting sash handles on all the upstairs windows' upper sashes. By 1984, Mary had grown fully into her role as Nauset Light Keeper's House owner, manager, resident, point person, and matriarch, with an ever-increasing appreciation for both its magnificent location at the dramatic cliff-side interface between land and sea and its longstanding, historical affiliation with the Lighthouse.

Monday, February 13, 1984: *This bedroom window out here at the Lighthouse must be where David stood when he wrote, "This is the day which the Lord hath made. Let us rejoice and be glad in it." At 6:30, the sun began to emerge from the cloud bank at sea-and-sky-mingling and by 7:00, it had made the whole east view like one giant photograph somehow* *trapped in the continuing flash of a flashbulb; it is so brilliantly misty all across the horizon. The only sound is the perpetual insistent syllable of the tide repeated over and over and over with only the tiniest variations in timing... outside, that is. Inside, an equally comforting repetition keeps me in my own suspended state: that of my two faithful retrievers who lie across my bed and me, their stomachs filled with breakfast and their coats shining with inner light as their slow and similar breathing carries them away to unknown adventures only hinted-at by the occasional twitch of a leg or a jowl or eyelid. It's as if time has stopped, resting, deciding what turn to take us in today. And we three lie here and wait too, happy that the decision for once doesn't even seem to have anything to do with us. Take us, Day. Take us wherever you will. Just give us a minute to find our tennis balls and our binoculars, then lead on!*

With Mary's encouragement and at her invitation, a steady stream of family and friends began to visit the Keeper's House. Mary's five brothers and their families came out over the first few years, and for four of them, it turned into an at-least-annual family event, long term. Friends Mary had a-plenty. Her natural love of people and her gregarious and generous nature expressed freely in the many facets of her life positioned her as a natural ambassador for the Keeper's House, leading to many of her friends and acquaintances also being invited to visit.

During this time, Mary paid close attention to each person's experience, initiating a Keeper's House logbook in 1982, into which each visitor was requested to make an entry commemorating their stay.

The Keeper's House Log became a fixture over the years, from 1982 to 2023, filling seven volumes with contributions from hundreds of people, all in some way connected to our family. Through frequent submissions of her own, Mary used the Keeper's Log to provide potentially useful information on local activities, restaurants, beaches, outings, etc., as she evolved into a kind of maternal overseer to all Keeper's House visitors, even affectionately signing many of her passages as "Mother."

"Mother" also took frequent advantage of 3M Post-it notes, on which she would proffer advice or direction on how to operate or maintain a particular item in the Keeper's House, and for operations about which she harbored strong feelings. At times there might be as many as 15 yellow Post-it notes stuck around the living area, usually laced with humor and hand-drawn emojis, etc., but always quite clear in their intended motivational purpose.

11–18 August 1984 (Keeper's Log): *The first Sunday morning supposedly dawned, but who could tell — the fog was thick enough to cut with, let's say, a chainsaw. Which reminded me, as I reread all these folks' testimonials to the universal appreciation of this fragile outpost surrounded by natural wonders we never asked for and rarely if ever deserve, that I should* *mention that one of the best ways to get your perspective restored out here is to take an hour out on a Sunday morning and go to one of the local churches. My favorite is the curious, genuinely Cape Cod "Church of the Holy Spirit" in Orleans at the corner of Rte. 28 and Monument Rd. Tucked into the pines and resembling — with its weathered shingles and its open-beamed, low ceiling interior — more an antique home (or the below-decks of a ship) than a traditional church. They thoughtfully schedule a service of Holy Communion in summertime at 5:30 p.m. in consideration of those who'd rather sleep in on Sundays; be forewarned that there is no music at the 8:00 service. The edifice is even worth a tour during the week as a point of historical interest. The book in the Cape Cod collection outside the downstairs bathroom here, called "The First 50 Years," makes fascinating reading: one learns that the church building is a patchwork of salvaged material — a piece of the old Higgins Tavern where Thoreau stayed overnight in Orleans in 1849 as he began his writing of <u>Cape Cod</u>[4] the intact galley of the clipper ship Orissa, which foundered off Nauset Beach in 1857 while en route from Calcutta to Boston; tons of timbers from the old Chequesset Inn in Wellfleet, which was destroyed in the winter of 1933–34 by shifting ice 12 feet high in Cape Cod Bay; a fan-light over the front door from Beacon Hill; a 250-year old ship model of a sailing dory made by Dutch seamen, in gratitude for being saved during a sea storm... The church's Galley West shop, open daily in summer, sells crafts made by parishioners, especially items like the hand-wrought aluminum plaques which decorate the sanctuary. Mentioning this may sound like "preach-ment," but it's only meant in the spirit of a story I read recently in The Cape Codder about William Beebe and Teddy Roosevelt who used to go outside on a clear night at Sagamore Hill, stare up at the Andromeda and recite: "That's the spiral galaxy of Andromeda. It is as large as our Milky Way. It is one of 100 million galaxies. It is 750,000 light-years away. It comprises 100 billion suns each larger than our own." Then TR would grin and say, "Now I think we're small enough. Let's go to bed."*

Looking back today to read guest log entries from the 1980s, the multitude of authors include family, extended family, personal and family friends from all aspects of life's time and experience, college alums, the retired, the young, some newly married, widowed, divorced, some who tapped into the blessedness of the place to become engaged or married, and others whose lives had left them reeling, or feeling at least temporarily "beached." The professional diversity of identity of the guest manifest reflects the gracious abundance of Mary's personality — counting within its registry entries from ministers, writers, engineers, executives, actors, day traders, professors, artists, actors, some unemployed and struggling, others thriving, friends and family from other countries (England, France, Finland), and even a couple of holocaust survivors.

Many of the elders from that period have now passed on, and some of the youngsters from that era are now in middle age or older — the younger family members having evolved to become the mature middle-aged or retired adults today who've maintained a regular visitation to the Keeper's House over these past 42 years. Most all those who've visited have shared a few thoughts in the Keeper's Log prior to their departure, some entries mundane or verbose, others succinct, thoughtful, expressive, informative, humorous, but all colorful and beloved, and all sharing a common sentiment of heartfelt gratitude and witness to what had been a singularly remarkable experience during their past few days as Keeper's House pro tem "Keepers." Often they were variations of a common simple theme, expressed as follows, in a couple of particular, early messages.

4 November 1984 (Keeper's Log):

Dear Friends,

Here we became reacquainted with ourselves — with each other — and with nature. We thank you for three days in Paradise.

Love, Ilsa and Peter

And in this one:

I came here saturated, I am emptied

I came here empty and am filled

I leave here new, breathing

I fly away...

– Doreen

Ironically, the environmental peril posed to the Keeper's House — and its perceptible impermanence — cast a stark backdrop of parallelism to the instabilities in Mary's own personal life during this period, rendering the Keeper's House seemingly at times the more stable entity. Her marriage was straining to the point of break-age, and her ulcerative colitis was beginning to worsen, further threatening her health. As 1984 merged into the mid- and later-1980s, the Keeper's House became an anchor in Mary's life, one of the few places of true comfort and respite for her, a frequent connec-tion point with beloved family, and a touchstone of relative constancy.

As she wrote in her book,[3] *"In those end years of my marriage, from 1982 to 1986, I ran to the Lighthouse as often as my responsibilities and my strength would allow. Once settled in for a week at a time, here on the edge of the earth, I drew enormous, if illusory, reassurance from the pres-ence of that tower just off the front porch. As its unwavering light revolved ceaselessly in the darkest and foggiest nights, it seemed to illuminate my personal darkness, and calm my sense of being at sea, of navigating single-handed the difficult course of the divorce negotiations."*

And yet, the momentary illusion of cliffside permanence in any one single day was being undermined (even literally) by the inexorable action of the surf over the course of a week or a month, as the reality of the visionary challenge she had accepted in her acquisition of the Keeper's House began to take on a materially perceptible form.

Sunday, March 10, 1985: *Arriving at the Cape cottage, I am instantly caught up in the trail of tasks to be done, as always. I feel like a shortstop at spring training whose team's rookie pitcher is getting shelled, as they say. An arm's length of tasks anticipated, compounded by the equally long list of "surprises" which always await me... First, there was the three cardboard half-gallon containers of Light-n-Lively (ha!), left by some all-too-generous renters. This neglected ice cream died by excreting all its sugar and alginate in a caramel-ish syrup which resembles pine tar or old varnish dregs and is about as fun to remove. Then there were the new residents to meet, the ones who scurry about in that telltale "stop-action" motion only a mother red squirrel could love. I drove the little devils out with a combination of The Police's album "Synchronicity" at near full volume, whacks on the walls and ceilings, and the dogs barking after them. (But later, when I closed them out with shingles cut from aluminum flashing to block their exit hole in the sliding-door coat closet, they chewed beneath them to re-enter)... Then, unloading foodstuffs, I found a strange gluey wax coating on the butcher block countertop which Fantastic only made worse. Mr. Clean, with his ammonia, cleaned it off as I scraped with a big chef's knife.*

It is so astounding that each time I arrive here, there is a whole new set of mysteries to solve, breaks to fix, misplacements to correct, cleaning-up-after to do: sand in the master bedroom closet, bricks in the patio to reposition and shore up; the no-trespassing sign which I hung from my across-the-driveway chain is nowhere to be found; et cetera, et cetera... And then there's some of the same old stuff too: gas indicator in the red-sector, so who knows if I have enough to last till they deliver Wednesday; the access driveway to the garage continuing to sink; the cliff out past the Light even more abbreviated, with large chunks of this winter's edge a quarter of the way down the face, holding on to what soil clumps it can with its tenuous root-grip, just until the wind and rain and gravity haul it down into the salt stratum where it will die the slow death of simultaneous poisoning and starvation.

Everything here is built on sand, literally and figuratively, and I always assume a kind of jut-jawed survival mode of thinking and working when I'm out here. All ten fingers in the dike sometimes and still feeling the tide of time rising, rising slowly but surely, over my boot tops.

I often wonder what will become of this wonderful house when its "lease on land" runs out sometime 20–30 years from now. Where does one move a big old heavy-as-the-brick-and-mortar-it's-insulated-with house, three stories on one side, two on the other? It's a mystery to me. I suppose I will always own my 429 feet of open beach. But someday the house will have to go, the Light will have to go, and my worst fear is that the U.S. Coast Guard, our most underfunded defense arm, will either do without a light here, or replace it with one of those 21st century fiberglass "hideosities" that serves only to send out a radio signal and maybe, just maybe, a light of some sort — the kind you see on towers near airports, which flash their electronic lights like some laser with hiccups, utterly devoid of history, beauty, or charm. I don't know. Maybe it's time to initiate a conversation with Jim Killian, head of the National Seashore...

Meanwhile, what a joy to find refuge from the crazed metropolitan world I live too near back home, and what a menu of days: some warmish, some freezing, most sunny, but just enough rain to give me an excuse to stay indoors and play with my own new toy, a Macintosh computer. I never really ever want to leave, but this time it's the hardest it's ever been. It won't be another three months before I return this next time, I guarantee that. "Carpe diem," she said to herself, noting the ever advancing-toward-the-light cliff-edge. "Nothing lasts forever," Mother said. And she's been pretty consistently right with that one.

By this point, the integration of the Keeper's House into Mary's life had become complete. She had developed a full understanding of both the privilege and her responsibility therewith as she'd assumed it — and had pretty much come to grips with both. At the same time, it was one of several foci of energetic intensity in her life — this, one of the stronger positives that helped to balance negatives relating to health and marriage. The latter two realities had together spawned a gnawing and growing awareness of the absence of immediate family in the traditional adult form, of a reliable love partner, children, etc. This in turn gave rise to a distressing sense of being somewhat alone.

Through her journal and logbook entries, one becomes privy to the evolution of her own perspectives on her personal life and her committed relationship with the Keeper's House.

Tuesday, November 12, 1985: *Cape Cod... at last! Outside this window, the surf crashes as if it knows something more than I — and the radio weathermen all up the East Coast — do. Somehow "showers and 50°F" and "partly cloudy" seem like whispers drowned out quite literally by this terranivorous beast that stretches from here to England and Spain and back. In the night, it is blacker than the sky ever was, anywhere, and when I look out at it from my bedroom window at 11:30 p.m., I feel as cold as the bodies it has distributed from a thousand wrecks over 200 years along this shoaled coast. The cold starts in two places: first fingers and toes and then from somewhere more central and figurative, and if I stand here long enough, the two cold fronts will meet, I'll turn ash-grey, and my pulse will stop... Death by imagination... I've waited so long to be where I am... and — No, I want to be here alone, and all the conjured-up memories about who was happy to be with me when, and where, and how it felt (some of those remembrances are so clear as to be almost palpable) are only so many islands in the stream of my life that is mostly cold and black and roaring and erosive... So be it. I'll just amuse myself with mental movies wherein the soundtrack is Rachmaninoff this week, as I BE MYSELF, MY LONE AND HAPPY TO BE SO SELF... So, stay back from the foot of my cliff tonight you insatiable ocean: I'll see you in the partly cloudy morning when you've had the night to think it over and can thus be more civil.*

Wednesday, October 29, 1986: *I begin one of those fast-walk days that somehow metamorphoses into a marathon-run day by trying my hand at painting using a $0.95 box of watercolors found in the Stop & Shop stationery department yesterday. On Sunday, I revisited the Wellfleet pier, where I first and last tried this (the result of which, a sort of Grandma Moses-using-a-mouth-stick picture of the clock, hangs in my garage at* home). I can see I haven't received The Gift yet, although Grandma seems to have regained minimal use of maybe two fingers of her "expression hand." But when I became an adult, I put away my $0.95 toy paints and, seizing the larger hardware store variety, I painted all the windowsills and the front steps and porch floor and washed windows; then I finished rigging the driveway "gate" and cleaned out the garage, did a load of laundry, ate dinner, and thought I'd never be able to walk again — this must be "middle age" because at times like these, it actually feels like I have one foot, knee, and hip in the grave!

Fortunately, I was able to stay awake through "Shadowlands," the BBC movie about C. S. Lewis' marriage to the American admirer — the "Jewish atheist communist" whose alcoholic husband runs off with his secretary, leaving her, Joy Davidman Gresham of New York, and her two young sons far better off even if they _were_ broke, living in a new country, and she about to be diagnosed with bone and breast cancer with maybe a year to live.

I have only known Clive Staples Lewis through his writings, wherein he seems to have It all Together, though he is free with his stories about how he used NOT to. But in this chapter from his life, I have come to see him as a weary fellow traveler, still burdened by doubt even as his faith is at times so strong, in between times when it is shaken to its core. He draws an analogy between faith and learning to dive — essentially that in diving you don't learn to DO something so much as you learn to STOP doing something — meaning fearing, controlling, "figuring it out," following reason. You just LEAP.

He was plagued by a nagging fear that what he'd come to believe would turn out to be a myth, a lie. He spent much time alone, even when with others (as he was not a hermit); but instead of characterizing his solitude as "hiding," he called it "seeking." When his wife dies he fears his own grief — that his suffering, as hers, will turn out to be "just suffering — no pattern, no purpose; just pain in a world of pain."

There were so many lessons in his life — in just this short chapter of this man's life:

"A friendship is not a small thing, but it shouldn't be turned into a watered-down version of something it isn't (meaning 'love')," he tells Mrs. Gresham one night as a way of laying everything out on the table so she won't be hurt by her unmet expectations.

Ah, yes. And Mrs. G. says, "All along I believed that somewhere there was a home for me. I had to wander into all those houses to find it, (she thought perhaps she finally had, but he resisted) and believe me, I wandered into a lot of wrong houses."

His final observation about feeling his leap to believe had led him to a closed and double-bolted door makes him ask, "Was the door bolted on my side, by my own too-great need?"

Life as a house. Life as a home. Each time it seems so apt an analogy, it is shown to be a misleading one. The one recurring truth, which each of the characters is on the way to experiencing, not just believing, is...

"THIS IS JUST SHADOWS: REAL LIFE HASN'T BEGUN YET."

And no, it doesn't make sense. It's not supposed to. The things in life that do are making only transient circumstantial sense: no conclusions drawn from them will prove to be THE truth that could spare any of us the pain of the journey to life's end, or prolong the joys we find along the way beyond their time.

I needed to see this movie. Mary will keep all these things in her heart and ponder them. She will from time to time share them with others who may be helped by them. And when she herself needs to recall them, *she will hope there will be someone who can gently point them out to her without placing too much emphasis on the obvious fact that once, at one time, she seemed to have known them, for she wrote them on these pages.*

Outside my window the stars are bright enough to shine even through the Lighthouse's white beam; there are three distant fishing boats on the black Atlantic; the tide is retreating, in no hurry, with no drama in its incessant rushing noise. The lighthouse has stopped its infernal squeaking. The sills and the porch and the steps continue to dry, being spared the predicted showers. And I have packed away the shortwave radio, knowing there is no music in this world as conducive to sleeping as that being performed this night just outside this window.

It seems so compulsive to leave tomorrow morning. Someday I shall live here. I come closer and closer to seeing that as the probable truth... or, I should say, A probable, circumstantial, and temporary truth, no less a joy to look forward to because of all those qualifiers.

Horizontal nexus of beach, dune, sky and ocean.

Saturday, November 8, 1986: *Painter Anne Packard of Provincetown says of her stunningly evocative land- and seascapes: "Horizons... they are very important to me. Oftentimes, though, I just miss the horizon. I leave it out, leave it to the viewer. I let people find their own." And of her seascapes' attraction to viewers and purchasers — especially the storm scenes full of power enough to take one's breath away — she remarks quite rightly: "People love to experience that, the drama without the danger."*

Yet not knowing where the horizon is is a kind of danger, isn't it? I recall the confounding and, at the same time, always suspected truth that my friends and I "discovered" two weekends ago as we decided to walk up the outer beach "just till we reached that bend" — "that bend" which always beckons with a distinctive light that seems to have come to rest right THERE between cliff edge and water edge, in a mist that is not only brighter than all the clarity about it, but also contains colors found nowhere else around it, in front of it or on either side. But when one attempts to walk into it, it recedes continually, tantalizingly, and from a great unbridgeable distance. It is impossible to even measure that distance — it advances beyond one, a step at a time. Misty Sisyphus.

Wednesday, March 25, 1987: *At the Lighthouse! I've washed the thick coating of sand off the east-facing window here in the master bedroom and now I can see through it — the encrusted crystals of sand had made the window opaque, translucent really, and even when clean, the sand has left the panes randomly etched so they sparkle with tiny pinpoint scars of the winter's raging storms, which evidently carried more than just snow in their teeth.*

The tide continues its race to the shore into a westerly headwind, which will shift again later and bring us, by late tonight, rain. I see — just above the brown pine tops and bare brush — long thin bulges like growing tucks in the water. As they near the beach, they fold over themselves, and as they do, the westerly wind blows their leading edges to bits and flings them back over their tops into the flat brilliant dawn light. Called "horse neck" waves, these are so long that at times in the width of a window's worth of these rollers, I find three of these salty steeds in a photo finish, their manes of slightly different heights, as if this were an open, all-age, high-stakes race...

I brought my 1980 birthday present out here to its new home, a Zenith Transoceanic radio with a bunch of shortwave bands (on which I heard radio Moscow last night interviewing street-folk from Kiev who told how much they loved their city and so much looked forward to their "usual spring weather, mild temperatures with occasional snow" [!]). This morning I'm listening to the initial 5 minutes of Robert J Lurtsema's famous program of classical music, "Morning pro Musica," from WGBH Boston.

Keeper's House living room, northwest corner.

The first 5 minutes is always unsullied bird songs and as I listen to the speaker on my right, I think some of the living things on my left, 100 feet outside the window, are too: they've suddenly come alive and seem to be answering the recorded northern woods-edge crowd with their own songs. Birdsong stereo, and what a breakfast it is. The news of the sixth straight record close on Wall Street seems very, very distant, thankfully. I must say, that after walking up to the cliff edge yesterday and finding it ever nearer, I am inclined to begin seeing a move from this idyll — fragile as it is, and ultimately representing a real preservation challenge — as a prudent idea. After a couple of months of marathon challenges, I'm plain old tired of them; I'd very much like to find a path that connects points of <u>rest</u> rather than challenge. I don't apologize even to myself, for what may be perceived as wimpishness. I've paid my dues and now I'd like to enjoy some of the membership benefits please-thank-you-very-much. I think I'll use this place a lot more this year — this summer — than I have in past years. August is still blank in the rental book. I think the family ought to link up and live here, family-to-family, that month and recapture some of that old Truro-cottage spirit again before the chance is gone and I find another person such as I was — a starry-eyed romantic with sea-water in her veins — to buy this historic outpost, bravely guarding the eroding cliff even as it

49

creeps ever nearer, ever faster. It'll fetch a pretty price, this place — and I'll be able to live with that if I sink it into perhaps another preservable Light-house/Keeper's cottage on more solid footing. And yet... I am captain of my own days here, this time, and what a relief; what a foreign feeling. I could be in another country and never know it...

Irish writer Robert Gibbings, in "Lovely Is the Lee," a used book I found yesterday in Bourne, says, "Listen. Listen again... Stand by the tree and think yourself into it." It's what I'm doing just now, turning off the radio. Out here, at the edge of the dry land, I can hear, for a blessed change of tune, the sea's endless line of percussion sounds, with a low hum — now soft as if silent, but then rising in volume if not pitch, as a comber meets its match on the long flat beach. The birds, when one is tuned into the sea's song, are a dry descant in comparison. There is no music like this anywhere else in my life. And it makes me wonder if ever I'll be able to recapture it elsewhere if I should decide to sell this place.

Of cairns, Robert Gibbings writes, "All the grand monuments in the world tumble away, but a heap of stones lasts forever." And this on the day after the ghost of lighthouses past was uncovered again by the outgoing tide down on my beach: about a dozen courses of brick tall, the ring — a section of one of the first "Three Sisters" towers — is visible several times a year, a stalwart survivor in that uncompromising relentless tidal wash. I wish that the mason who joined those bricks were alive today to see what his work has withstood: first, The Fall, and now 100 years of twice-daily tides.

Beach remnants of original Nauset lighthouse foundation
(1990).

Saturday March 28, 1987: *With randomly blown rain-shot peppering my window on this wet world of ocean, clouds, and showers, I leaf through my collection of thoughts and impressions gathered here these past 4 days. I note, first of all, that before this in my life, I would be stalled on the single unchangeable conclusion that 4 days spent here is like 4 pages torn out of the Book of Questions and handed to me without answers: maddeningly incomplete. Now, I still feel as if I'd like to spend more time here, now that I am here, but I see that I have willingly chosen to move on. I wonder, if I weren't committed to head for New York tomorrow, would I be as ready and willing to leave? Maybe. And I say that because there is a new sense of choice operating in my life these days, now that I am out from under what seemed to be a blizzard of circumstances, making me the REactor not the ACtor in my life during January, February, and half of March. I also note that I am seeing this place a little differently this time: not as much as something requiring me to sacrifice for, to lie in front of the bulldozer of geologic time and an ocean's voracious appetite for crumbling cliff-feet — but instead, as something somewhat evanescent, here today and gone tomorrow. There used to be almost suffocating sadness in the reality of the limited life span of this place. Now, I'm more accepting and circumspect — and bully for me, someone who goes for a walk, deliberately leaving coat* *and hat behind as she steps out into the slanting rain and comes back a half-hour later soaked to the bone and — wonder of wonders! — not exclaiming at all about the fact that she's cold and wet. <u>This</u>, my Self, is real progress! <u>This</u> is to write home about!*

Somewhere around this time, Mary's writings begin to reflect an emerging recognition of the formidable nature of the steadily more imminent challenges and responsibilities embodied by her private ownership of the Keeper's House. The complicating factor that all the property surrounding the federally owned lighthouse was also privately owned (by her), gave rise to its own set of tensions, contributing to a sense of exasperation expressed by Mary in her journal and in the Keeper's Log — as illustrated in the next few excerpts.

Wednesday, August 5, 1987: *@THE LIGHTHOUSE!!! Bad enough to arrive here and find the road up the street permanently claimed by the ocean, and folks running around in front of my "NO TURNS" sign in my driveway, but to find many books missing (most from the Cape Cod and Lighthouse Lore sections) and no notes, a bag of trash in the garage and no backup trash bags, and every sink in need of scrubbing... landlording is beginning to take its toll. Judging from the rental ads in the Cape Codder, I am not charging too much; I think I have simply been putting up with too much. A letter to renters will go out when I return, another "Mother wants to know" missive bearing threats and begging cooperation. Funny how life conspires to make one a mother even if one has no children.*

In half an hour, a woman reporter from the Cape Cod Times will arrive and ask a lot of questions about (I quote) "All the interesting things that happen to people who live in a lighthouse." At the very least if I go along with her idea, I shall remain nameless. I considered the idea of acting the part of a crazed recluse still mourning the death of my father, the last lightkeeper; but that's fraught with another peril — I'm afraid it'd make this place an even more attractive focus for curious tourists. And that'd mean eyes peering in the windows and other forms of being "poked wiv a stick" than I am already subjected to.

Friday, August 21, 1987: *Among the week's best/worst "touroid"**
remarks: "Well, my little 4-year-old boy has always wanted to have his
picture taken in front of the Lighthouse. If you won't let him, I sure hope
you'll be able to explain it to him."

* Mary was always gracious and friendly in encounters with
passersby, but she reserved the term "touroids" for those relatively
few inconsiderates who would tromp right past the "Private Property – No Trespassing" signs in front of her house to (often arro-
gantly) stake a photographic claim to her backyard or back porch.

The *Cape Cod Times* article published August 19, 1987, entitled
"Enduring Tourists Is Cottage Industry," describes the problem.
"Imagine walking onto your front porch and finding a group of
strangers sitting there, chatting away, and taking pictures of each
other. Or having those strangers knock on the door and ask if they
can come inside to use the bathroom. For the family that owns the
cottage at the base of the lighthouse at Nauset Light Beach, this is
the kind of thing that goes on all summer long. People trudge onto
the property day after day, insisting they are on public land, despite a
roped-off driveway and signs that proclaim private ownership and
warn against trespassing. The problem, according to Mary Van
Roden (owner), is that people don't realize they are on private property. They insist it belongs to the government, and therefore to them,
she said. The truth is, it doesn't. (...) Mrs. Van Roden told of a recent,
persistent woman who found it hard to believe she would not be
allowed to walk up to the Lighthouse. After listening to Mrs. Van
Roden's oft-told tale about private ownership, the woman asked
how she would then be able to get onto the 10 feet of land (surrounding the Lighthouse) that the government owns. In frustration,
Mrs. Van Roden suggested a helicopter."

Also in August 1987: *The beach became covered, during the full-moon*
tide Saturday night, by all the brown algae that had made the surf so
unattractive for swimming last week. The high tide ran all the way to the
foot of the cliff, and when it receded and the sun had baked the beach all

morning, we found mats of the dried algae all over the sand. And it's still there today, layers thick in some places, so it lifts up in foot-square pieces and separates like thin laminated cardboard, and falls away in big chips. This beach is an endless source of wonders. How could I say I do not want or plan ever to live here full-time? I can't.

Final full day of the Cape Cod height-of-the-season vacation experiment... and a full day it was. The high point was the 3:00 p.m. high tide, during which we stood around the lifeguard chair in awe, experiencing the awesome force of 6–8 foot waves that came all the way from a tropical storm near Bermuda to reapportion the sand all along the outer beaches here, and to drive the hundreds of sunbathers and volleyball players and beer drinkers and boom-box addicts all the way back to the cliff to escape the enormously high tide. I awoke this morning to a strangely noisy surf for a clear day, and it turned into this hurricane-like tide in stunningly gorgeous weather. At peak tide, a young girl and several others, standing too close to the bank of sand the breakers were carving out of the beach, were suddenly swept out past the waves — maybe 150 yards — and were obviously unable to swim back in. These were the kind of waves that will knock you down and then, as you begin to regain your bearings and grab for a footing, they knock you silly and haul you farther out. The red-suited lifeguards raced into action: it took the first one no time to reach them, because he went in where they had, and he too was swept out to that no-man's-land. The second and third men had to swim as if uphill <u>and</u> against a tide to reach the group with two life-floats and one long rope, the other end being held by a crew of three back on the beach. It took 20 minutes to get the swimmers to shore, and their final exit was the scariest live action I've ever seen on a beach. For a moment it looked as though a couple of them would never be let up by the sequential crash in waves and their fierce undertow.

This evening the waves parallel the beach perfectly and break not only at the shoreline but, as all day, 200–300 yards out too. This tide will probably follow the extent of the 3 p.m. one: it will reach the foot of the cliff and create a near sea of backwaters and a far sea of mind-boggling power and persistence. Not hard to see how the Cape has spent all its life slowly disappearing...

Wednesday, March 2, 1988: *I'm sobered by the continuous stories printed in the Cape Codder, the twice-weekly newspaper I get from Orleans; they report how the folks along Andrew Harding's beach in Chatham are responding to the loss of a hundred or more feet of their shoreline property to the waves now coming through the mile-wide breach in the Outer Beach which began last February in one of those great storms. Research has shown that such a "cut" existed there 100 years ago, but it was gradually filled in by the sand redistribution that constantly accompanies the longshore current the incoming Atlantic sets up when it reaches the Cape's forearm. The first responses were to throw up some kind of barrier, rocks, boulders, sandbags, a constructed, engineered revetment. But the voices of land and resource management and conservation, in reasoned opposition, sent the matter to Boston to the courts.*

One house has now literally fallen over onto the beach and had to be bulldozed out of its (owner's) misery. The next day President Reagan got around to signing a bill, part of the Federal Emergency Management act, that — from that day on, but not one day back — would provide some kind of monetary compensation for future homeowners whose homes were eaten by the ever-advancing tides. (Pictures of one home lying all atilt on the beach made me wonder why no one has salvaged "parts" from the structure, let alone moved it out of harm's way even to a temporary site, before it was on its way to smithereens. The sight of nice trellises up the west side of the place, and the shutters decorated with small wooden seagull models, even the intact gutters and downspouts and screen doors and window frames, made me aware that nothing is NOT disposable anymore. A mere year is not a long time in which to lose your house, but it's long enough to salvage what of it might still be useful in reconstructing it somewhere else. Can I picture an Indian not moving his tepee out of the way of a forest fire, and instead petitioning the tribal council — or the Bureau of Indian Affairs — for compensation to build another because he didn't move it?)

Anyone who's bothered to read any geological account of why we even have a Cape Cod has to know that it is ours for only a short period of time, geologically speaking. By ~2988, it may well be all gone, just as Billings-gate Island on the bay side in Wellfleet is now all gone — and that only 50-some years ago. Just as we ourselves are put here for our 75 years (average) and can be said to be winding down, running out, dying from the instant we are born, so is Cape Cod: it's been being rearranged out of existence from the moment the glacier retreated and the leftover ice-mountains melted, raising the ocean level.

So what's all this fuss about a little more consequential — but really no more persistent and steady — reclamation of the ocean side of the outer Cape by The Guy Who Put It There In The First Place? It's His to do what he wants with. "Nothing lasts forever," my Mother and my Creator said, both, almost in unison.

"Therefore will not we fear, though the earth be removed and though the mountains be carried into the midst of the sea." (Psalm 46:2).

Through the term of Mary's private ownership of the land surrounding the lighthouse, and up until the Nauset Light Preservation Society (NLPS) assumed management responsibilities for it, the Lighthouse was serviced and maintained periodically by the U.S. Coast Guard. On several occasions, it was possible to enter the lighthouse under the supervision of ANT (Aid to Navigation Team) members, who were always well mannered, friendly, and respectful. In one instance, they were invited into the Keeper's House by a guest, and asked to make an entry in the Keeper's Log, which they chose to address to Mary directly.

25 May 1988 (Keeper's Log): *Hi, my name is Ron (–and Milt). We were here 25 May 88. We are with the U.S. Coast Guard. I think I met you last year while painting the Light. You are a fascinating woman! I could have listened to you for the whole summer. I was here visiting the Light once again, and again it's beautiful. Wishing to see you again this summer — Milt USCG*

Saturday, the Foolth of April, 1989: *AT THE LIGHT!! Getting here was NOT half the fun. And a bit like the pony in the manure pile, I know there must be a lesson in this trip, somewhere. I think I was near Newark when I realized I had not brought the keys to the cottage. It was a dark thought that summoned my Emergency Response Thought Center to work. Forget the rain, forget the stupid dumb drivers in the hammer lane doing 55, forget the ear-crisping racial/sexual dialogue on the CB radio — time to find a way not to have to turn around and go back to Malvern for the keys sometime in the next six hours. I remembered three sets of keys along my path: one with friends in Stratford, one with friends in Guilford, and one with my house watchers in North Eastham. Surely one of these groups of people would be home so I could call and stop by to borrow back the keys. WRONG! None of these folks were at home. My last idea was to find out from my friend John how to use a credit card to break into a house: I was going to stop and return a book anyway and John's a clever fellow with a checkered past. But he wasn't home either. So I continued on, resorting now first to thoughts of which windows were less likely to be locked and how long a ladder I would need to reach them, and second to prayer. Visions of either slipping off the wet roof trying to enter through the upstairs bathroom or being arrested at the top of a ladder to my bedroom played and replayed themselves in what was left of my brain, and in a fit of enormously strengthened (by enormous desperation) faith I began to pray. I recalled Mary Walmsley's line "The name is 'Jesus' and the word is 'help'." It sounded too easy but there were no longer any alternatives, save a 7-½ hour return drive to Malvern. I began imagining going to the patio birdbath, raising it and seeing a set of keys there amongst the grootz and the grubs. That seemed too easy, too, but the investment of time and thought and faith now just about approached the value of such a reward, and I thought of it as being paid-for and hence deserved.*

As I rounded the big bend in Ocean View Drive down by the old Coast Guard station, God eclipsed Nauset's bi-colored beam with a blast of total-sky lightning of enormous electric-blue-white proportions. Meaning! There had to be a meaning: is this the sound made when God creates keys? I hope so, because it is also the sound made just before God creates torren-

57

tial rain, and I suddenly had a flash-image of me being struck dead by lightning and washed off the roof by a Noah-sized downpour.

There was an eerie quiet as we got out of the car — and one last tantrum, as I couldn't find my flashlight (it was sensibly stowed, by me!, in the glove compartment). And then we three road-weary travelers were out on the patio lifting up the first birdbath and seeing a set of house keys glistening in the flashlight beam.

I got down on my knees and said the doxology, crossed myself, wondered if I was facing in the correct direction, and we came inside... just as the skies opened up and all the water in the atmosphere came cascading down in my yard.

Monday, April 3, 1989: *I have not walked out to the edge of the cliff yet. I'm afraid of how short a walk it is becoming. I've eyeballed the distance, from up here at the bedroom window, and I guesstimate it to be maybe 100–120 feet yet.*

At the 60-year average of 2.95 feet per year lost to the ocean, that seems comforting until I remember that nobody but me and the Coast Guard are

counting — and one of their ideas of solving the problem is to let the tower go over the side just like all its predecessors. (I wonder that people back in 1890 actually watched the set of three lights descend the cliff — I don't suppose they all fell at once in one big gravity demonstration. What did the onlookers feel? What change did it make in them, seeing an aid-to-navigation succumb to the very forces it was warning seafarers about? It would have been like watching The Good Guys surrender! I <u>know</u> that people of today would shrug and walk on by, because they've seen <u>It All</u> by now, and the collapse, at whatever speed, of another of life's intended but outdated reassurances is nothing new — Life, such as it is, goes on, regardless.)

Some wonder why I don't cash in, find a rich buyer, take his/her money, and run. I hear myself tell them I view it as a responsibility to work to save it, something I'm sure I will do and that I "owe" Miriam and Lou Rowell to do in their absence: to champion the saving of their dream-spot. I also feel that because it was bought for me, it wouldn't somehow be right to cash in and run. I hear myself say these things, and I do believe them. But I have a sense that there are other quarters inside my head and heart perhaps not heard from yet... They have a few more years to speak up or forever hold their peace. I wonder what they have to say. I wish I had a hint...

Tuesday Morning, June 13, 1989: *AT THE LIGHTHOUSE, which is receiving a new coat of (this time) the Right Color Red paint. Last time the Guard did it, they picked the Wrong Color Red — a dark, matte-finish brick red that made it look war-painted or, less imaginatively, merely primed and waiting for the finish coat. The new Right Red, now applied only in one two-story vertical stripe so far, looks positively gaudy over the other, but once it's all done, it will once again be the Big Red — the Big BRIGHT Red — we all have grown to love.*

I guess I've never been here at this blooming-time before, because during my brief reconnaissance walk around the yard I found things pushing up flowers in places I didn't even know there were "things." The irises on the ocean side in the tall grass are red-earth color with bits of white and blue and yellow in them; those on the street side, again in the tall grass (where I never saw them), are bright blue. And several Japanese irises survived the soil disruption, resulting from the patio reconstruction. In the grass on the west side, grass that's in some spots a foot tall, some snow-in-summer — usually kept clipped by the mower to a pre-bloom height — is now bedecked with its snowy white flowers making me think I should transplant it into the garden where it won't have to continue to bump its tiny head on a lawnmower blade.

In the corner of the garden by the garage, where it joins the house, is a nice tall gorgeous rose bush all decorated with lovely mid-sized puff-ball-like yellow blooms. I thought that corner was all filled with holly — I can't remember there being a rosebush there — certainly not one 6 feet tall! The rugosa roses are doing fine too, not only looking lovely all covered with pink and white flower-dishes but perfuming the air as well. As I unpacked the car, I kept walking past several petals lying in the grass and when I was done, I bent down and got one (amazed at its texture: like a thin kid-leather glove) and put it over my nostrils as I inhaled the warm air. What a trip! Canterbury bells, chive flowers, spurge blossoms... it goes on and on from my window. Here the cliff looks nearer, as always, and the mid-strength roar of the incoming tide seems too near. But over and above its percussive dance rise the songs of maybe six or seven bird species who are just as glad to be here as I am — they can't be more glad than I, who am looking forward to, they say, two days of rain-leavened work in the yard and patio, putting in the hundred different annuals and perennials I brought up from "Malvernia" (reference to home in Malvern, PA), which seems even more than hundreds of miles away from this edge-of-the-earth idyll.

...and next morning...

The mockingbird holds on to the windburned top of the scrub pine — halfway out to the cliff edge, looking cold and wet and having every reason, this rainy morning, to grumpily cancel his/her performance. But instead, he sings every other bird's song for him/her, even the "WHEEEE-ah" cry of the gull, rotating his/her head to fill all of this wet patch of creation with song — even the gray white-capped ocean that merges into sky only a short distance out.

One curious note: at about Dennis on Rte. 6 yesterday, I discovered that I possess the ability to warble, at long last, on about a range of 5 or 6 notes. (I don't know their names.) A Vibrato! The same ability I have both admired and despised in others, and which I have proudly not exhibited <u>and</u> secretly coveted, going so far at times as to ask Them What Has It how they "do" it. It's always seemed to be easy for them to do and impossible for them to articulate-about. I have always come away believing it is one of those things that if you have to ask about how it's done, it ain't gonna happen for you. You have to sit back or stand around and wait to find out if you're standing in the HAVEs line or the HAVE NOTs line... all the while NOT thinking about it. Curious, this is. Maybe Vibrato is a gift of the Spirit, one of the ancillary ones not mentioned in the Bible. In any case it, like mustard, is to be used sparingly and selectively. As I witness whenever my friend Harold, aka "Wagner," joins our tenor section and unleashes his voice from behind his ruddy British face, a little Vibrato goes a long way, and you can die from too much of it. Mine I will keep under a bushel, thank you. I'll fool with it in the car on long trips, maybe it's just visiting, and without being unfriendly about it — I know I "got along without you/Before I met you/Gonna get along without you now..." (Thanks Patience, Thanks Prudence)...

The Advance of the Sea Toward the Lighthouse

Date of Measurement	#Feet: Edge to Light
4/16/88	94
10/29/88	94
7/8/89	94
11/4/89	93
1/13/90	92
12/1/90	92
2/9/91	89
6/13/91	87
11/2/91	79
4/23/93	72

Source: Eastham Department of Natural Resources

Mary's Private Ownership During Erosion Crisis (1989–1996)

Monday Morning, July 10, 1989: *Sue B told me that on Saturday the shellfish/natural resources/police officer who appeared on the Nauset Light property came to take the semiannual distance-to-the-cliff reading — a record I had no idea was being kept. This time he found 92 feet separating the lighthouse from oblivion, showing a loss of two feet since eight months ago (November). In the six months prior to that the reading showed 4 feet of terra had become "infirma," so in a little over a year, I've lost 6 feet x 429 feet or 2,574 square feet of my once 3.95-acre (1981) — and once 5.2-acre (1923) — property. Time to apply for a tax abatement at the least, not to mention to start requisitioning an outer second line sandbar from God to replace the one that evidently got away recently, leaving my idyll twice as vulnerable to the onslaught of the tides. Six goes into 92 entirely too few times for my peace of mind. I guess in 15 years, in the summer of 2004, my 60th birthday may find me either supervising the moving of my historic pair of landmarks or using the base of Nauset Light as a pier to which to moor my sailboat.*

Sunrise, Friday, January 12, 1990: *The sun has to rise over a thick cloud wall at the watery horizon, burning off the top before blazing over it. Now that it has, and it seeks me out through this east window, I am surprised anew by its energy, warming my bright red corduroy wrap and me, giving, giving, giving, and all I must do is receive, soak in it, be amazed at this engine that runs the terrestrial machinery without issuing invoices, requiring no maintenance or husbanding: a free gift, like the saving grace its inventor also shines down on our calculating, stubborn, stingy heads.*

Up here, out here on the edge of North America, the things that I read fall on a ground more well prepared than ordinary daily ground. It's as if everything has an aura about it, a halo, a second image that illuminates its space and makes my eyes linger longer as if to lap up the least little bit because I need the nourishment, the enlightenment. A little reading goes a very long way: I am so filled with the feelings the foreword-ist has written about Breece Pancake's stories that I have to stop, to wait till there is room, to read more of them. I bought the stories of Breece D'J Pancake in 1983 which I've looked forward to reading "someday," but I could not have gotten what I've gotten from even the mere foreword, until I had lived my life to "now" and had the experiences I've had to prepare the ground.

Through the 1980s, all of Mary's siblings (Joe, Andy, Tim, Peter, and Steve) and their spouses and young families spent time both with Mary and independently of Mary at her Keeper's House, beginning to build memories that have lasted a lifetime. My own children have been visiting annually since birth in the mid-80s, along with a half-dozen of their cousins, all of whom have grown up to become fine young adults (Alisa, Heather, Ben, Cass, Joey, Jake, Lydia, and Robbie) — several having formed their own young families since 2001 when Mary passed away.

Many of Mary's friends and sometimes <u>their</u> friends visited as well, with Mary occasionally renting her house or allowing folks to spend time on a barter basis, in exchange for the performance of essential maintenance work like painting, mowing, refurbishing, repairing, etc. As various folks would visit, they would usually want to come back again, and thus would begin a family legacy of summer vacations by which children would fall in love with the place and want to repeat the experience over and over.

The guest log chronicles these visits in a manner that makes for delightful reading today, these many years later.

April 1990 (Keeper's Log) (Amanda, in young person's script):

Dear Mrs. van Roden, my mom doesn't know I'm writing in this, but I have to tell you what a great time I had on our first whole day. I woke up to see the lighthouse right outside the window, it seemed, and that wins the cake for the best view to wake up to in the morning. Mom has been really stressed lately, and I think this is what she really needed. There is a great view of the ocean, and even though today was cold, the walks on the beach were fantastic. Well, my mom will probably yell at me for writing in this so soon, but I want to thank you for owning such a wonderful place that gets you away from everything but yourself!

P.S. I saw the map of all the shipwrecks right offshore… any ghosts??

And then later (also, Amanda):

It's me again, our second night we got a really big storm, with winds strong enough to shake the beds that are upstairs, but I think the lighthouse really came in handy.

We may go up to the Visitor's Center. We already found a couple of starfish and nice shells. The birds here are beautiful. My friend I brought would like to say a few words…

Then in different handwriting, her friend:

This is a really beautiful place. I've been to Cape Cod before but I've never seen anything like this…

Among the more frequent visitors during this time were Mary's good friends Jim and Sue from Connecticut, who loved the place and were very interested in coming out to help Mary with servicing and maintenance needs while combining Keeper's House business with the pleasure of an oceanside stay. Mary very much appreciated their efforts at a time when her poor health and her challenging schedule afforded her insufficient opportunity for trips up from her home in Pennsylvania to the Keeper's House, and through this early, mutually beneficial exchange arrangement, the three of them forged what was to become a lifelong (though all-too-short) friendship.

About them, Mary wrote in the **Keeper's Log, July 1990:**

Oh, the modesty of my friends Jim and Sue, who are hereby named Chief Assistant Lightkeepers of this venerable station! The reason they wrote so little in the book is because they had no energy left after their work week here in June. We all have them to thank for the clean rugs, floors, windows, newly painted radiators downstairs, the view to the shoreline from the window-seat windows, and best of all, for the eviction at last of the red squirrels and the patching of their last access-hole in the south wall.

And, from her journal, one morning at dawn that same month:

Why does the catbird sit in the top of the scrub pine each morning and sing every possible bird song known to it — and probably some it makes up? Is it pre-emptive? ("I knew that. Why, I already said that this morning before you were even awake!") Or is it a wake-up call to all the other birds? ("Hurry up and look alive before someone else sings your song for you!) Or is it just oral aerobics, so no matter what song might be called for on this new day, the catbird will be able to sing it? Or maybe during the long dark quiet night, the catbird's song center has gone right on manufacturing songs and storing them in its throat, so the very first thing the catbird must do each morning is let all those beautiful songs out before it bursts!

There is something missing here. Has been for all the time I've been alone and sick. I just hope it's not another person. I feel very too old and tired and settled in who I am to even think about being someone full-time for someone else... or is it someone else full-time for someone?

As we grow older we become more like who we are — who we've always been, underneath all the roles and pretenses and costuming and posing. I'm not unhappy with who that is, in my case, but I surely don't want to even think about whether or not that is someone that someone else might want to live with, or even spend time with.

No. I am a discontinued product. If anyone wants one, they'll have to take it as they find it — no instruction manual, no spare parts, some pieces missing. And they get to "take it" only if the present "NFS" sign gets removed. And I'm holding on to that today with all my might.

By 1991, Mary had been divorced for several years and continued to suffer with health issues, particularly ulcerative colitis, which, although somewhat debilitating, did not unduly limit her active participation in her life. With her parents having relocated in their retirement from southern Connecticut to Lyme, New Hampshire, and two brothers with young families pursuing careers in New Hampshire and Vermont, Mary decided that the time was right for her to plan her exodus from the Philadelphia area to move closer to this northern focal point of her birth family. Over the course of 1991–1993, she found a desirable piece of land in Lyme, New Hampshire, and constructed a beautiful new home on a hill with 17 acres of natural woodland, that she lovingly referred to as her "aerie." During its construction, she found herself spending more time than previously accustomed at the Keeper's House.

Friday, February 15, 1991: *The morning dawns bright, the long-lost sun burning out of a calm sea. The air is cold and the sound of an incoming tide washes my ears and eyes of the accumulated resignation to the penetrating dampness of two days' rain and snow.*

It is the new moon, first day of Chinese New Year, the Year of the Sheep... Yesterday, the Acorn Homes rep. came down from Concord to spend a few hours nearly finalizing my house plans. It was a productive meeting. Now I have only to close my eyes and I can walk through the place mentally and know it will be an exceptionally nice place in which to live. I will surely be very happy with my Acorn home on Acorn Hill. It almost seems predestined.

To plan one very expensive house while staying five days in another during a mini-vacation from a third seems reprehensibly egregious. But I am selling the third to pay for the first... that's 33% less egregious, no?

I will leave here tomorrow with some tasks still in need of doing: the screen door has blown off the Oil House, the master bedroom's sash cord is busted, I've got to find a painter, and critters larger than mice are living in the walls again. As toasty and warm as this fortress is in these wintry gales (with the midnight snowstorms that animate the lighthouse beam with pointillist crystals), its skin is holey as Swiss cheese, allowing entry probably at points I can't even see to these four-legged furry tenants I can only hear.

I confess that I am increasingly looking forward to my relocation to a new state; a new house, a new start, a new slate as a chance to slough off old skin in a way — divesting myself of all that has held me back and down, and freeing me to rebuild a new, light, flexible me so I'll feel again like living to be 93.

{I'm listening to the solo flute of Masahiro Arita (playing 2 of 12 flute fantasias by Georg Philipp Telemann) on the radio and what I find most fascinating is not the sound emanating from the instrument (made in London in the 1700s) but the sound of the flautist breathing in, in between those long lines of notes strung like pearls on an almost inaudible strand of air.}

Out here where I can watch the sun rise out of the ocean just there (she points)... and less than a day later, watch the same sun sink slowly into the bay just THERE (in the exact opposite direction) — it seems such a small globe, this earth. And East and West seem so near; and the floating sun at midday somewhere up above but not at all close enough (she pulls her coat closer to her thin skin), seems just THERE (upward) almost within reach... This is the illusion of a narrow land, that, holding its thread of ground against the forces it illuminates and, for a season, buys time from, and as it warms, seems to have an abundance of what it will soon lack in sufficiency. It is a grand and resolving equation and it makes me feel at once caught up in it and wholly irrelevant to it (she admits and sighs)...

Friday, April 26, 1991 (weekend): *No sounds in the walls this morning. No flicker drumming. Still a lot of squirrel discord out in the bushes around the patio. One pre-dawn scratch at the new aluminum shingle outside the*

window but a hasty retreat via gravity when I raised the sash for a better look. And one barrel-belly raccoon who upended the smaller of the stacked feeders and then sat around eating a pound of seed before wallowing down the hill into the brush.

Bird songs and surf sounds both increase as the pink sky brightens to blue-white — the turning tide barely makes the effort at shore-line down past the Nauset Light beach stairs, but out at the first sandbar, a line of wave break gives the shallows away... and probably because there are no such protective sand deposits off my beach, the surf sound is local, right at the foot of the lighthouse cliff.

I did walk out the path the other afternoon, to see for myself if the erosion has been much worse this winter. I went slowly, not really wanting to reach the cliff, eyes down, noticing little blue vinca flowers in the way underfoot. Where the path angles left — a point I well remember though I do this trip only once or twice a year — I looked up and saw that the perhaps 12–15 feet of cliff-top where the path used to straighten out due east again is not there anymore! I didn't go near the edge, as the bowl-like cut in the normally straight north-south dip looked quite undercut, but I could see the cousins of these little vinca plants halfway down the cliff face, still singing the same blue song though now 30 feet closer to death in the crush of gravity, wind, salt air, and rain.

At the bottom of the cliff the ankle-and-foot of clay-and-rock amalgam stretched out uncovered into the tide, and, a little farther out was the brick ring that was one of the Sisters' hemlines a century ago. I remember that ring, some 12 courses tall, being right at the foot of the cliff six years ago!

"Enough!" my spirit said sadly, and I turned my back on inevitability and returned to the illusion of terra firma at the base of the Light tower.

Monday, April 29, 1991: The dogwoods are abloom, speckling the woods with small clouds of petals suspended in the new green sea of the under-brush's tiny leaflets. All down the front hillside (this first spring after the clearing of the swath of trees that blocked the view into the woods) are blooming Virginia bluebells and Jacob's ladder, and garlic mustard,

70

brightening what looked all last summer like a clear-cut slashed hillside, brown with the chipped remains of the "trash trees" I had cut down: mulberry, sapling walnut and ash, and all but two sassafras spindles — even a dying dogwood. The hillside feels healed now, and the wildflowers are returning interest on the investment of sweat and sunlight. It's a new and welcome addition to the many beautiful views from this house's windows and porches, whenever I stop going-to-somewhere-else long enough to Be Here Now.

In her original book,[1] Mary explained in "Part Three: Vicarious Light-Keeping," that she lived pretty continuously at the Keeper's House from August of 1991 to March 1992 with her dog (Clipper) and cat (Mew), after the sale of her home near Philadelphia and during the time her new home in Lyme, New Hampshire, was being built.

Mary's journal sketch of old lighthouse foundation ring exposed at low tide.

Saturday, September 7, 1991: *How stabilizing a thought to know that one's parents and grandparents are/were "good" people. It insulates one from the potentially destabilizing thought that who one is and what type of person one is or will be is not connected to anything at all, but instead just develops like an image on a blank sheet of photographic paper in a tray of chemicals mixed by no one one knows.*

How lucky I am to have known all four of my grandparents, and both my parents, and all their siblings — so I can know, to some degree, that I come from a type of home and family two generations back with which I identify and for which I am thankful. I used to think I could become anyone or anything — in a childhood unlimited by anyone else's imposed ideas on that subject, all futures were possible. But what if I had had doubts about the track down which I came — what if there were, early on, evidences of instability on either side, so that at any moment I could be blindsided by

71

unknown realities popping out to block my path. ("_You_ can't go down this path — your grandfather was a murderer." "You can't be here, your mother was a prostitute.") It might be equally unnerving to simply not know at all who or what one parent or grandparent was or is. To have been adopted might have been a derailing shock requiring support from unusual sources to withstand.

My own life has been so blessedly protected. It has held no shattered tragedy, no gaping lacks, no deforming experiences — and ample strength and self-image to handle what disappointments and detours and bad decisions it _has_ held.

How can someone so ordinary (or is it extra-?) with so little drama in her life ever hope to write anything that others not so blessed would ever want to read? (Who can compete, for drama, with the Philadelphia Inquirer or the New York Daily News?) I honestly do not know what I have to say that will be of more than passing interest to anyone now living in this same hyperstimulated world I do.

Sunday Night, September 22, 1991: The moon looks full tonight, illuminating the surf and showing the Lighthouse that constancy has at least as much to recommend it as color changes and occlusions. I think tonight marks a change of season, summer to fall, and thus another excuse to sit still and quietly review what has changed since the last equinox. Perhaps it would take less time and effort to review what has NOT changed, I think... And then I decide against _any_ backward glances at all and instead sit quietly and commend myself on an excellent decision not to think at all. This place is so blessedly quiet. And it is so good to be back in my own home again instead of on the road.

Tuesday Afternoon, September 24, 1991: Sitting in the sun under the Lighthouse's steady gaze (it's looking far beyond _me_!). "_Mens_ barely _sana in corpore_ quite _malo._" I've just spent 40 minutes carting dirt from the well site up the hill to fill in the trench the rain has re-excavated a bit, raking and tamping and getting a headache — surely evidence of anemia (or some worse reason for no oxygen reserves to handle even mild exer-

tion). I am certainly in terrible shape for doing more than I usually do: errands, sightseeing, long and short car trips, schlepping my bags out of one house and into another. I am skinny as a rail, so I don't <u>feel</u> out of shape. But if I ask myself for 40 minutes of manual labor, Manuel, he say "Mañana!!" I keep telling myself I will start going to my mother's ancient-persons' exercise class and I'll join the CCB pool when I'm relocated. But what if I die of wastage before then? Well, then a lot of my family will be somewhat financially better off than when I was alive, and my estate can skimp on a child-sized casket. (No crypt, please. The worms won't find much to eat anyway, so why keep them out?)

What a Cape Light day this has been! In the sun, it's maybe 78°, T-shirt weather to be sure. The surf sounds gentle, the sky is a marly wash of blue and wispy white, the grass here in "Lou's lawn" is as green as it can be, giving the moss patches some color competition. The "solar-collector" dog lolls at my feet, rolling in the stubbly grass and holding a stick in her two forepaws above her smiley mouth. There's a daily-enlarging list of deferred maintenance chores on the kitchen table, but they all seem eminently deferrable on a day like this.

Hurricane Bob, with all his mega pruning of three weeks ago, actually has produced a strange positive effect on the flora of this area: the autumn olives are putting out new foliage, tight bunches of spring green leaves, the Rosa rugosa is doing the same and blooming to boot. I read that some folks with fruit trees are seeing a second flowering, so there are, on some trees, blossoms <u>and</u> ripe fruit, a highly unlikely coincidence under normal circumstances.

I feel a bit weathered myself and yet I know I'm coming out of that and into a bright new beginning, even as autumn arrives and winter lurks just beyond the color. Lucky Me to have unwittingly taken a cue from post-Bob Cape Cod and — through no effort or merit of my own — been given permission to at least green up and maybe bloom again, if not to set fruit. (Thank you, Jesus.)

Wednesday Morning, September 25, 1991: *The day holds only the promise of more wind and rain, at seven in the morning. The brave scrub between me and the insistent ocean shakes and protests the wet wind it seems to get underneath its cover. The only positive side I can see from my ocean-facing window is white-caps directly offshore from my property line, well beyond the beach, out into what is usually deeper water. The transient sandbars that caused them are one more (of 2) positive gift from Hurricane Bob. Perhaps because they are there, tripping the waves early and causing them to give up some of their force before shore, my 429 feet of cliff edge will suffer less erosion this winter — last year's 12-15 feet of loss will not be welcome again for a long time in these parts. If the average annual loss is 3 feet, I would hope for a year of* <u>no</u> *loss and then a gradual return to 3. But no one has asked me, and my preferences are lost in the sighing wind that curls around my sturdy house and swirls out to sea.*

Friday Morning, October 4, 1991: *Out this window this dawn can be seen a relatively calm ocean — or is it just unusually organized? From the distance of its calmness develop slim stripes of waves running the entire length of — and perfectly parallel to — this outer beach, one after another, all of the same size. So that when each reaches this shore — this ever nearer-to-me shore — the roiling impact is heard all along the beach, north and south, at the same run of moments. One particularly intense wave took about 10 seconds to unburden itself, and during that time, the wave noise was all RIGHT HERE, not disappearing up or down the beach away from me.*

Yesterday I explored the northeast corner of this property where my land (how odd that phrase always sounds, and how uneasily said) meets the neighbor's land (that is oddly easier to say... why?). I found that out in that corner, the cliff edge seems/is even closer than down farther, near the lighthouse, where I usually assess it. Next time I go down to the beach I will look up to the pine tree I've noted, standing like a sentinel very near the edge, and note whether — as I suspect — when the neighbor's front yard went, all in one winter, maybe four years ago now, that enormous patch of sand also extended into my property, too, and I just never noticed it. Odd not to "notice" the land you live upon disappearing. I'm sure this is my lasting incredulity at work, saving me from thinking about the disaster which ultimately will be no longer ignorable.

This summer's well replacement, I think, signaled the beginning of that end. When this next well fails, for any reason, and the only remaining alternative will be to revive the cellar cistern or live on bottled water, I will have to have a plan (or 2) for the property's eventual disposition and the obtaining of another plot for this venerable house and its unusual lawn ornaments (Lighthouse, Oil House) to be moved to. I've given this subject much thought, but I have never sought out local advice for fear of tipping my hand and allowing too much time for public reaction to the boldness of my proposition: that the National Seashore, in exchange for my beach-front, give me a 99-year lease on just enough land nearby — and farther back from the cliff-edge — to set the house and the Lighthouse and Oil House on. After that, perhaps the buildings would revert to public owner-ship and access, perhaps as a Lighthouse museum (such as Ken Black's in Rockland, Maine).

I can see how beloved this proposition would be in the current backlash against the costliness of open-space acquisition here in Eastham and neighboring towns. My plan would be a lot less costly, as I could donate the fair market value of the land and be satisfied with a significant tax deduc-tion potentially extendable over the rest of my life (?). My father would not be happy with the plan, as he thinks I should even now be looking for that Arab sheik who wanted to buy the place from Miriam back in 1981 and stick him with its future, walking happily away with a million bucks in cool, sandy cash.

Monday Night, October 7, 1991: *The temperature is to dip to 40°F tonight, so I spent some of this day sprucing up, pruning, organizing, and reuning with my house plants which have spent these past five weeks out on the patio recovering from the move from Pennsylvania. I've brought them into the sunny cellar, assigning them to various windows, shelves, and even Miriam's old sewing table to begin their acclimation to indoors again. They all look a little the worse for wear — some LOTS worse — but* *all have enough green left, after pruning dead stalks and leaves off, to give them a good chance to survive this last shortest displacement, 20 yards and 20 degrees from where they last rested.*

I just noticed that DANGER is an anagram of GARDEN and GANDER. (And also of NEDGAR. But so what?)

There's no moon out in that icy velvet black sky anymore. I thought that would make it easier to find Cepheus, The Sunday Times constellation of this week. But when I looked — at about 9:30 — for some reason I couldn't identify anything in the plethora of pinpoints the Lighthouse beam kept dusting off for my viewing pleasure. I had gone out to a new restaurant in Dennis with friends for dinner and was looking forward to getting to bed early to read, so I didn't persist in deciphering the dots. Instead, I aired my old romantic fantasy out one short time — wouldn't it be nice to have some wonderful available man point out to me all I ever wanted to know about the night sky? (sigh) — and then I did just that: went to bed to read.

Thursday Morning, October 10, 1991:

And where does a monarch butterfly spend the night? Although they migrate along this shore in enormous numbers, they are so distant from each other that each appears as an individual — each on its own in defying the updrafts at the cliff edge that not only provide necessary alti-tude but also threaten, as they meet the clifftop prevailing wind, to blow the ultralight long-distance flyer off course — deep inland or out to sea. Such valiant travelers, all dressed alike in Halloween colors, in material so fragile that alighting askew on a clifftop shrub could mean an early end to what seems to me an endless attempt to get somewhere before something worse than the journey itself intervenes. The pointy foliage of the ever-greens where often a monarch alights (to rest? to survey the course ahead?) seems as potentially consequential as a bird's confident pause on a 20,000-volt power line. It says volumes about our differences — ours and the other creations passing through "our" world in "our" time — and all of it humbling.

"A sense of humor helps to smooth the sharp edges of life and tends to moderate the ego."

— *Nan Turner in "Journey to the Outermost House"*

Yesterday I heard news of the second stranding of pilot whales on Eastham Bay beaches. (There were three such episodes last fall, and this year we are just two weeks into the 6–8 week "stranding season" according to Henry Lynn, our natural resources officer.) There is in place a standing alert procedure, which calls to the scene experts of all kinds, and trained volunteers, to minister unto the mammals until they can be moved out into the bay again. Fewer each year (as a percentage of those beached) die any more, thanks to these folks. But no corresponding increase in knowledge about why pilot whales do this has occurred, despite the taking of blood samples from — and performance of autopsies on — nearly all the whales who do not survive their plight.

No one has asked me. No one is likely to. But if they did I would muse aloud about the even minute possibility that the whales do this to escape and to protest to us humans about our persistent fouling of their natural habitat. As they continue stranding on our shores, some millions of dollars are being spent to construct the 9-mile-long, 24-foot diameter "outfall pipe" from Boston out into the Bay these whales call home — a tunnel intended to bear the liquid and solid waste from the toilets of 42 Boston suburbs and the city itself, minimally treated. It's the most ludicrous "out of sight, out of mind" plan I've ever heard.

Could the whales be telling us something we already know but yet refuse to acknowledge? Is our taking of blood samples and body sections as off the point as if we did the same to those radical right-to-lifers who beach themselves in front of abortion clinics? Maybe instead of looking through a microscope for the message, we should be listening through an ear trumpet, or asking John Lilly to translate for us. I know it's far-fetched, but it may not be inapposite to view these unwanted suicidal visitors in our backyard as negligible, abusable, dispensable life-forms because we can't think of a better place to dump our body waste than into their habitat.

Wednesday, October 23, 1991: *Back at the Light after 10 days in New Hampshire. Last evening when Clipper and I arrived home, a note greeted us from the tenants describing the things that had inexplicably "just broken themselves" during their stay, two of which we'd already found: the longitudinally bisected lower tread on the porch stairs and the double snap for the cross-driveway chain which went from "working" 10 days ago to dead now: broken at <u>both</u> ends (with no evident pieces to rebuild it with). Inside there were patches where spilled stuff was kind of smeared around on the floor rather than being "rinsed-up" — some yellow gunk — and terrible toilet paper in every holder, and hide-and-seek to play with the kitchen paraphernalia and a house full of dying-of-thirst or drowning-of-overwatering plants. Oh, and the kitty-food dish encrusted with 10 days' worth of turkey-and-giblets leftovers, the dish never having been washed between feedings. Upstairs all the throw rugs were in new places, one put underneath the blanket chest at the foot of the bed: why? And two of the four lights I turned on had burnt-out bulbs in them.*

Again I am confronted with my love-hate relationship with some of my renters. Yes, they reimburse me somewhat for maybe 50% of the costs of holding the place together for our enjoyment. But they also treat it (with few exceptions) like a rented cottage, any old rented cottage anywhere... At least they don't steal from me.

Nauset Light at sunrise, view from Keeper's House living room east window.

This morning as the near-full moon dimmed and colored itself in the pastel western sky, sinking into the pine tops at 6:59 a.m., the sun rose out of the orange-purple-gray pastel sea horizon, and this glorious 65° day began.

It is good to be home, where I have all the elbow room I want and the accompaniment of the ocean on this endless shore to carry me along through the day, and the night. Filling the bird baths in one large feeder (with use-it-up supermarket-quality seed) has brought a bevy of finches, sparrows, jays, chickadees, and a few critters of the chipmunk persuasion to the patio. Seems too warm to be coddling them with store-bought food. But November is just a week away and then they will need my handouts, as much as I will need their flittering, cheeping presences to brighten my days.

Thursday Morning, October 24, 1991: *I know what is so compelling about being here at the edge of this hemisphere: it's the simplicity of the land-seascape. Last evening at sunset, Clipper and I went down on the beach and watched the full moon as it rose transparent out of the ocean and slowly gathered color (a pinky rose) and then turned solid white-ivory as it gained a place in the darkening gray-purple sky. Looking north, up the endless beach, the swirl of blue mist that obscures the distance where cliff and sand meet water, darkened and disappeared. Down the beach not another soul could be seen. Clip and I were the only 'peds in the 'scape and I wanted, like Clip, to bound and leap and cavort in sheer delight at being undiscovered, undestined. HERE ALONE WITH ALL CREATION IN THIS SINGULAR MOMENT that seemed sustained like a breath all around us. In a landscape like this one (and like a desert or prairie or snowfield) one feels one can see everything there is, and without directed vision: one simply perceives it all at one look. If anything moves or changes, one will be sure to see it against all that is simply **not** moving or changing. I think I could suspend myself in the sea-present forever and not get older, not have another thought, not care if anything else ever happened in my life until God tapped me on the shoulder and called me home.*

JAWBONE ON BEACH IDENTIFIED, *the local newspaper headline grabbed my attention. "The human jawbone found on Skaket beach in Orleans late last month has been identified to be that of a Wellfleet fisherman who apparently fell overboard and drowned in March 1989,*

80

according to the Orleans Police Department. The fisherman's boat was found aground on the Brewster flats March 24th, 1989. It was assumed that the fisherman, at the time of his death, fell overboard while clamming in Cape Cod Bay. The search, which included two boats, two Coast Guard cutters, and a helicopter, was abandoned during the days following the accident due to hazardous weather conditions. The jawbone was discovered last month by a couple visiting the area from New Jersey. They reported the find to the Orleans Police Department which in turn referred the case to the State Police Crime Prevention and Patrol Division, in charge of all intelligence on missing persons. Ten teeth on the jawbone made identification possible through comparison with dental records."

I wonder if it is somehow better to confirm your husband's fate with a tangible bit of evidence like this 2-½ years after he disappeared; or to imagine him whole somewhere but unable to return. The discovery of a jawbone — the one bone that carries with it a row of ID marks — is a wonder: how did it and it alone come ashore just two towns south of the fisherman's home port, Wellfleet? It's almost like a message from beyond his watery grave whose currents and depths and other life forms claimed and devoured the rest of him, sending just his corporeal ID card back as if in thanks for having received him. And just a week before All Soul's Eve. It's uncanny and sobering and leaves me with more, excessive, evidence that we are in no way in charge here on this earth we think we have subdued.

Mary describes the days of Monday, October 28 to Thursday, October 31, 1991, in Chapter 3 of her original book.[1] It was during this time that the area was hit with the 4-day "No-Name Nor'easter" which was considered one of the outer Cape's "storms of the century." So as not to be redundant, Mary's published recantation is not repeated here. However, not included in her original relating were a few of her in-the-moment thoughts and observations, described in her journal as follows.

Monday Night, October 28, 1991: *Late at night, the wind still hasn't let up. It shakes the house in this bed as I sit up against the other side of the* *north wall it's hitting. Between these displacing collisions, the whine at the windows, the hollow tube-like ringing of the wind around the lighthouse tower, and its rumbly growl — sometimes I imagine I'm on a night train, reading in an upper berth in a Pullman car shooting across the black prairie...*

The beach will surely have a new contour tomorrow. All week there's been like a bench the whole length of my section and down into the public part. Clip and I sat on it to watch the last of the moon rise a few days ago, it was that hard and that high. I hope all this wave action doesn't remove the long offshore sandbars that Hurricane Bob left me for winter erosion protection. The ocean giveth and the ocean taketh away... My feeble wishes are so much irrelevance in the face of its ultimate goal of removing this moraine from its path so it can get directly to work on the mainland.

Tuesday, October 29, 1991: *This afternoon's visit to the Nauset Light Beach public access finds the stairs roped off and 10-foot waves breaking near enough to send a foot of sea water and mocha sand-foam 7 to 10 steps up, to scour out more sand from the foot of the cliff — which is clearly gone. What's left is a whole new cliff foot, a sheer drop from about 10 feet up, where any minute what's above that will just crash down into the foam for lack of support. At Coast Guard Beach, I'm told the water is up to their stairs too — and that's way far back into what was just a few days ago cool dry sand.*

I'm glad I got the storm windows and doors up, after vacuuming about ½ cup of fine sand from each inside windowsill before fitting the storms to their interior magnetic tracks. The furnace has cycled on and off less frequently the second half of the day than it did the first.

At 9:30 p.m. up here in the bedroom the wind sounds more fierce than last night. The house flexes more, it seems, and in different places, so it makes different noises from those I am used to hearing. I think of water on stone and wonder if wind on wood has equally cumulative negative effects. The scant forecasts one hears on Cape Cod's primitive radio stations say it will be "windy" through Friday — that is, if anyone will be left to notice.

Clipper seems spooked by the noises. Mew interrupts her self-grooming now and then to stare at a ceiling-to-wall intersection that has just spoken. I think of my Bob-given sandbars offshore underneath that relentless sea that looks the same no matter what time of tide it is — I wonder if they will survive and serve a wave tripping function this winter (which can't hold worse erosion forces than these). Then I remember, as if I am my own grandmother, that "all things are but lent to us for a time." I also recall how ancient that thought and its ilk seemed to me just a few short winters ago. Just when I'd begun letting go of my dream to live to be 93, I start talking (to myself) as if I already <u>am</u>...

Wednesday, October 30, 1991: *Mother Nature has found a note she likes and she's driving me crazy with it. "STOP THE POUNDING!" Mother D'speck used to shout from another room when our too-percussive piano playing reached her cultured ears. I am thinking the same thing even as I hear on the radio that it's to continue, this windstorm, today and tonight and tomorrow, too. A meteorological data buoy at Georges Bank out in the Atlantic northeast of us is registering 50–70 MPH gusts and 35-foot waves.*

Sand is drifting like snow on the front porch, in the corners of the patio, on the windowsills between screen and window, even in the battered pink roses still valiantly abloom in the patio garden.

Awe turns slowly to irritation. Enough is enough.

Then I feel such a fool for reacting to the unfathomable vagaries of weather that swirl like runny icing around this spinning marble as it hurdles through space.

At about 3:30 p.m. I went up to watch the action down at the parking lot. It looks like drive-in church with the penitent scurrying about with bowed heads, mostly but not all covered. The incoming tide is smashing onto and up the beach to the foot of the cliff in towering waves that sometimes break upon each other at a slight angle making what looks like a volcanic eruption of water pitched high into the air and caught by the wind which carries it like a dense tan cloud up over the cliff and to the west/southwest.

I can see where, to the south of where the stairs were, the sea has made a hole in the cliff and is carrying another 100–150 feet inland toward a small gray one-story cottage. Outside on the street, a Park Ranger is stationed in a truck to keep the faithful from going up this side-aisle to where the road is probably impassable — and where, if one lost one's step, one would tumble to the roaring surf below with no hope of reaching land again until that maelstrom had had its way, rinsing the life out of the person as it has from all the pine skeletons that swirl below in the surf.

***Thursday, Halloween 1991:** Some roof shingles in the yard from the north ridge area east of the chimney seemed to be the only things the winds of last night removed from my house. Every window and most screens are opaque with salt and sand, but drying off a south-facing screen showed me (via binox) that Nauset Light Beach is at least 10 feet closer to the parking lot today than it was yesterday. Where two men stood yesterday afternoon watching the ocean invade behind a dissolved cliff barrier, there is no longer a spartina-covered knoll, and I wonder if the ocean reached the little gray one-story cottage tucked into the low curve of the plane there. If it did — or even if it established a foothold behind the cliff face — that bodes poorly for the stability of that whole National Seashore facilities area. Once breached, twice invaded... and worse.*

Up my street, where the road washed out a couple of years ago, the ocean took another 20–30-foot bite, spitting out a telephone pole with its wires still attached and leaving it lying on the beach 50 feet below. The Nauset Light Road section that used to extend beyond the old bite is now cracked as if it had been creased down the middle, signaling undercutting beneath it and significant instability. I didn't venture past the crack — if it gave way, there's no way up from the beach anymore but straight up the cliff. Going down would be a lot easier than coming back up...

Down at Nauset Light Beach public access, the stairs and part of the walkway that used to parallel the cliff edge 10 feet in are gone. Washed away. EXEUNT. The beach is littered with dead trees, lumber, lobster pot markers, shrubs, and a new septic tank regurgitated from the earth when erosion reached it.

Down at Coast Guard Beach the whole shore-scape has been totally changed. During the night, winds had pushed the 30-foot seas OVER the elevated, paved, heavily trussed access bridge, seriously damaging its understructure and spilling ocean tidewater into the salt marsh. Another storm like that and the Coast Guard station will sit atop an island surrounded by tidewater. The little brackish pond between the Coast Guard station and the beach is gone — washed out to sea. Past the Coast Guard station down the spit, on a barrier beach on which fishing camps (shacks) used to sit, all but three small, raised sections of dune are gone and they will be islands too in this next high tide around 5:00 p.m. The most stunning change, though, is where the ocean devoured the cliff — it wasn't a high cliff but it was a pretty substantial edge between the road and the ocean — and washed across the road leaving behind it its massive cargo of sand (from my beach, no doubt), turning the varied terrain into a flat stretch of incursive beach at road level. It looked a bit like a moonscape, it was so desolate and uniform.

For the next year or more, Mary's life center moved temporarily away from the Keeper's House with a few exceptions to include the occasional off-season visit and time spent during the summer with various factions of immediate family in 1992 and 1993. During this period, while settling into her beautiful new home in Lyme, New Hampshire, she took time to address some of her physical health issues (knee replacements and physical therapy, arthritis, colitis) with the help of specialists. She also bred a litter of retriever puppies, traveled a bit abroad — throughout Spain — and provided continuous support as needed to her retired parents who now lived just a few miles away from her in Lyme. Her heart and thoughts were never far from the Keeper's House though, and she maintained regular contact with friends on the Cape who were involved with the formation of the Nauset Light Preservation Society.

29 October 1993 (Keeper's Log): (After the first organizational meeting of the new "Nauset Light Preservation Society")

The trip down here in a wild nor'easter-wannabe, was like one I had traveling to Taylor Hall (Bryn Mawr) in a hurricane some 30 years ago for a final exam. I released and re-edited my case for preserving the Keeper's Cottage as well as, and (I hope) at the same time as, and to the same relocation site as, the Lighthouse. And when I got to the second meeting of the brand new Nauset Light Preservation Society, I was indeed called upon — by the head of the Eastham Historical Society — to tell why all three structures listed on the National Register of Historic Places (the Lighthouse, the Keeper's cottage, and the Oil House, too!) should be kept together. My recitation was well received and unanimously supported by all in attendance who commented. So, instead of a lone David facing a triune Goliath (the Coast Guard cum National Seashore cum Town Fathers), I find we are all in this leaky rowboat together, rowing like hell, and all in the same direction: toward a suitable relocation site, ASAP. What a relief to find unanimity where I feared animosity toward me, the private owner of the house next to Big Red. The next meeting of the NLPS is in two weeks and I'll be there with bells on.

And the presence, these last 2 days of good friends John & Ann made the trip a joy. They included me in their unplanned and serendipitous ramblings, from yesterday's gourmet feast at the Off the Bay Café (in Orleans, highly recommend) to today's detailed tour of the historic Crosby Boatyard in Osterville — topped off by a cosmic buffet comprising an extended sunset at Rock Harbor, a moonrise at Fort Hill, a highly percussive wave symphony at Coast Guard Beach, and watching the pups race up and down the moonlit surf line at our own Nauset Light Beach. We are so lucky to have this place at which to enjoy such times and such friends — It restores us to the simple pleasures we knew as kids and makes all of our life's appointment-filled days and weeks slip away awhile to let us be the happy children we were, and still are... if we will only allow it to be so.

The prospect of "simply" moving this whole diorama west a bit and restarting the clock is heartening. I can feel Miriam Rowell, the grand lady who entrusted this place to me in January 1982, watching and smiling and telling us not to worry...

11 November 1993 (Keeper's Log): *Another trip "To The Lighthouse" to attend the next meeting of the Nauset Light Preservation Society — which was well attended and featured multiple vendors of Nauset Light baubles, trinkets, and portraits offered as fundraising items: an excellent new twist on the exploitation of this cottage and its famous lawn orna- ment. (There was even a news team with lights and a video camera at the gathering!) It is continually amazing to notice that all these diverse factions (townspeople, Coast Guard, National Park Service [NPS] staff, vendors, and I) are together on the same side in this project — at this point, it would appear that all good things I've dreamed of for the three buildings comprising the historic Nauset Light Station are indeed possible — that they will all be relocated together (or can be), with public funds being used for the Light and my funds for the cottage. (I wonder how many dollars it costs to move an old house to a new foundation and sink a new well and septic system. I wonder where those dollars will come from, all at once, maybe within a mere year... The English major in me shrugs her shoulders and looks about for a math major to hazard a guess...)*

This morning, as we three (Clipper, Polly and I) watched the sunrise from the master bedroom window, we savored the sweet sound of the surf and drank in the palette of colors, as the cobalt blue sky with its fingernail moon and several shimmering stars began to pale eastward. We are so lucky to be here, to have HERE to look forward to, and now to know that our family and friends will continue to be blessed with experiences like ours out here at the edge of the earth for years and years to come. The last move back from the cliff edge, a distance of 200 feet in 1923, gave the place 70 more years: time enough for us to be included in the developing history. Maybe the next move — a much greater retreat, I expect — will allow Tim and Pete and Steve's own kids to experience this sunrise, this glimmering star-filled night sky... and, as we did this morning, this ever-present chance to romp at dawn by the surf's advancing edge.

Now it's time to pack and to head northwest to home, and to think about our return on or about December 4th for the Eastham Chamber of Commerce Christmas Fest, when they've asked the Coast Guard and me to open the Lighthouse and the cottage for the townsfolk to see what it is they will be preserving... Till then...

December 4, 1993: Some 200 very nice people marched through here today, during the open (Light) house feature of Eastham's annual Christmas kick-off. Two fine fellows from the Coast Guard's Woods Hole station came up and opened the Light tower and I opened the house — with the help of many stalwarts from the Nauset Light Preservation Society. There was a handsome Christmas tree atop the sea trunk in the parlor, a beautiful wreath on the door showing one of the new Nauset Light Christmas tree ornaments, candle-lights in every window, pine garland wound 'round the banister, Nauset Light suncatchers in the windows, my two blinking lighthouse models and a host of wooden and stuffed Christmas figures peering out from every corner and shelf. At dusk we mounted a floodlight in the autumn olive bushes out front, shining up at the Lighthouse itself, and from down at the parking lot against the navy blue sky, the whole place looked like a work of art. I've never decorated here for Christmas before, but now that I see how warm and inviting it, looks I can hardly bear to go home! The NLPS raised over $500 in donations from 1 to 4 p.m., not counting the "royalties" from ornaments, suncatchers, and Harold Jennings' book, which he autographed (in addition to providing lectures about lighthouse life gleaned from his and his father's and grandfather's experiences at various New England light stations... while wearing a vintage 1939 lightkeeper's uniform. His wife Hattie, dressed as a 1939 hausfrau, greeted everyone at my front door as if all were returning relatives.)

It was a remarkable day: I am glad we did it, and I'm glad it's over. It is not a little disconcerting to watch as perfect strangers of all genders, shapes, and sizes traipse through your bedroom and bathroom just kind of STARING at things as if you, the owner, were dead or something. I felt just a little bit dizzy (LIGHT-headed?) all afternoon, and when at last I found myself alone again here I couldn't help wondering if that (solitude) was even really possible ever again... or might some laggard suddenly step out of a closet or the shower stall hours — or even days — later?!

I may stay an extra day, if tomorrow proves clear and I can coax Conrad and Pam's son, the photographer, to shoot me a roll of dusk pictures of the house and the Light all decked out for the holidays. (Especially one of my latest invention: the Eastham Christmas turnip, made by marrying one of Art Nickerson's fine tubers with a leftover wreath-ornament stuck into its sweet heart. I wonder if they'd raise NLPS some funds if sold as pet-rock alternatives...)

March 28, 1994: *Brother Tim and I came down for the weekend to attend the latest public meeting of the Nauset Light Preservation Society on Saturday. This morning, Monday, we are meeting with the head of the Cape Cod National Seashore and their chief planner for a mere 45 minutes to listen and learn about the official complexities of what ought to (but can't, evidently) be a simple relocation of two houses (1 Light, one even lighter) to new ground.*

The NLPS (PO Box 941, Eastham, MA 02651), needs money and it needs it NOW. The land out front is dropping off at a terrifyingly accelerated rate now (about 30+ feet in 2-½ years.) and soon the big trucks and dozers needed to uproot the tower will not be able to come in to do the job. Please call Pam and ask how to contribute today. Buying ANY of the proliferation of Nauset Light baubles and trinkets is fine, but there is none so dear to the future of our refuge as a cash donation made NOW. **PLEASE CONSIDER THE ENLIGHT'***ened self-interest of a generous gift... Light-heartedly, The Keeper (3/28/94)*

Following a relatively uneventful winter, from April to late August 1994 there are no entries in Mary's journal but a number of them in the Keeper's House Log. When Mary resumed writing in her journal in August, she described this period as one of having "too much to write and no time to write it." With the many aspects of her own life, her challenging health issues, her in-person support for both parents — each having had separate hospital experiences during this time — and her involvement in the lives of her siblings and their families, she found herself running full-tilt on the treadmill of her life, its speed intensified by the heightening of the visibility of the threat to the Nauset Light Station by erosion, as the ocean carved its way noticeably closer. This is the period during which she really began to feel the acute edge of the threat to her much-loved Keeper's House.

Sunday, 15 May 1994 (Keeper's Log): Mary spent a few days at the Keeper's House with good friends from Pennsylvania, who were celebrating their 1st wedding anniversary and who (Sharon) included in their guest log journal entry, addressed to Mary, the following: *"I also feel so committed to seeing the Lighthouse saved. It must be preserved! I am so very glad that you, Mary, and Nauset Light found each other. I sense that both of you are here to help heal each other. Years of erosion take their toll on lighthouses and humans alike. The response is similar for both — if you can't put down roots deep enough to prevent further erosion, it is definitely time to move! You have done well in your efforts to preserve the Light; I'd love to see you preserve the wonderful stories you and your friends have to tell of life on the Cape!"*

Mary herself wrote, the same day:

*As for the week with old friends from Pennsylvania, it's always a joy to share this place with people, and this time it was with folks who had never been to New England before! We were emphatically **not** alone — not only did Joe L, USCG reserve, lighthouse preservation expert, enlighten the three of us on Friday night on lighthouse lore of the outer Cape, but on Saturday and Sunday we and the Nauset Light Preservation stalwarts shared this spot with two thousand other people **each day**! If I hadn't seen it, I'd have never believed it. From 10 a.m. until 4 p.m., strangers arrived, to queue up 50 at a time in the front yard to hear Nauset Light history from NLPS and National Park interpreters as they prepared to admit groups of 10 to the top of the tower, where two Coast Guardsmen told technical tales and answered questions before sending the group back down the 44-½ iron steps to reality again. Many visitors were townsfolk who'd wanted to do this for most of their lives, and last weekend and this weekend were their first opportunities.*

So passed Massachusetts Maritime History Week, when all the Cape's major light towers were opened to the public, some for the first time ever. Both weekends, the NLPS turned my garage into a Nauset Light gift shop, selling about 50 different kinds of trinkets, ranging in price from $2 to $200 and signing up new NLPS members. Saturday's elegant cocktail party benefit at the handsome Whale-Walk Inn on Bridge Road, was an extra bonus at which I met the new editor of the Cape Codder, our biweekly outer Cape newspaper — and got good specific advice about how to get my manuscript published. (I've written "A Personal History of Nauset Light, the 1875 Keeper's house, and the 1892 Oil House" — and whetted the public appetite by reading from it at the Eastham Historical Society's annual meeting two weeks ago.)

Also this trip, I enlisted the able assistance of a brilliant Osterville real estate lawyer to even the odds that the Cape Cod National Seashore will see granting this private owner a land swap as something to benefit not just her and her family and friends, but literally tens of thousands of people in the future. Just the realization that there is now for the first time an ocean view from the north kitchen window is enough to justify the expense of legal assistance. After these two extremely successful weekends of pleading our common case to 4,000-plus people, the NLPS and I are confident that these historic structures can be moved together, and we are renewed in our efforts to see that that <u>will</u> be the case.

I'm exhausted now. I just want about 24 hours of sleep...

20 June 1994 (Keeper's Log): *Another successful Nauset Light open house weekend is over — this one began with a bus tour of 47 people "doing" all of Massachusetts' lighthouses, directed by Wayne Wheeler, head of the 10-year-old U.S. Lighthouse Society in San Francisco. Our NLPS gift shop debut went well and, for the foreseeable future, will not again be in my boathouse.*

Meanwhile, a couple of good varnishing days enabled me to do "Kestrel's" (my Lincolnville lapstrake wherry) floorboards; and a recipe from Nauset Marine (vinegar and salt, in a bucket) helped me spiff up her cast brass oarlocks, anchor, and belaying pins. I even planted "random annuals" in the patio garden beds.

The Cape is now in full summer mode, a psychological change in the weather that causes everyone to move more slowly and focus on the deceptively tranquil ocean which seems to be taking some time off for bad behavior through the winter: we are down to 53-feet, measured from the Light — and far less at the north end of the property. (sigh) JOIN THE NLPS!!! Nothing can be done until THEY have enough money, and I am stuck until then...

P.S. the first roses of summer appeared yesterday in the patio garden

Roses bloomed annually in the patio garden (Left) and southeast corner of the Keeper's House, just a few feet west of the Lighthouse.

August 13, 1994: *Yes, it is disturbing that the sound of Nauset Light Beach surf is louder than ever before (a function of its gaining proximity), and yes it is disconcerting to find an ocean view out the kitchen window this season. But it is equally <u>en</u>couraging to see the proliferation of Nauset Light gee-gaws, the sale of which puts needed dollars into the slowly growing coffers of the Nauset Light Preservation Society. (Memberships $10/year, from NLPS, PO Box 941, N. Eastham, MA 02651. Please join — because this idyllic refuge cannot be moved out of harm's* *watery way until <u>they</u> have the funds to relocate the lighthouse tower itself.)*

Now it's back to my other base of operations in New Hampshire. Hope the subsequent visitors will understand about the defunct garbage disposal (still runs but can't chew), the run-on-toilet (first floor — gently jiggle its handle, as needed, or reach into the tank — not the BOWL!! — and reseat the plug), the reluctant-to-shut-the-last-1/4-inch refrigerator door (push it), and the terminally lethargic pilot light in the broiler oven (watch your fingers and hair as you try the 3-match booster ploy about 5 or 6 times to jump start it — Aaargh!!) All such things will be made better when the place is moved: for now, all my spare $ is going into the relo-fund, as the estimate is inching over $50,000 (for this house alone)... Long live the Light!

7 October 1994 (Keeper's Log): *Up at 3:15 in New Hampshire this a.m. Off at 4:30 to come down to give my speech at the Eastham Council on Aging's luncheon. (topic: "The Seven Ironies of Moving Nauset Light") then off again at noon to see about a new stove, en route to NYC and Pennsylvania, by way of Guilford, CT. (I'm getting too old for all of this peripatetica...)*

NEW DETAILS: 1) We now have yet another new Silverstone non-stick frying pan (w/matching griddle). DON'T USE KNIVES OR ANY OTHER METAL IMPLEMENT IN 'EM!!!2) The stove has a truly tiny gas leak from a pilot light. NOT DEADLY by any means. (It's been inspected twice to be certain.) But if you notice it and it is bothersome, crack open the pantry window for a little while — or turn on the exhaust fan in the range hood (via the round black dial to the left of the range, on the wall). Leave it on just a minute and repeat as needed.

Gotta go...(just as the thermometer hits 60°F in the Indian Summer sunlight~~~~)

Love,

"Mother"

28 December 1994 (Keeper's Log): *Well, we can kiss another neighbor goodbye! Today was the day Mr. C's cottage, just south of my property-line, bit the dust. Actually that's a rather dry western phrase... let's say that instead of being allowed to "float off into the sunrise," it was devoured by a metal dinosaur with a diesel fueled fire in its belly and an appetite for wood. I was awakened by the beast's back-up beeping and mastication sounds, and by the time the pups and I arrived at the site, all that was left was a cellar hole and a pile of wall sections being "smithereened" by the dino's iron beak.*

It was an arresting sight. Kind of brought me right up against all that a house really is: a big box made out of vegetable fiber. Why, just five or six years ago that place was for sale for $250,000! A retired guy who wanted to buy it called me to see if I'd grant him an easement for a driveway through my property down past the little garage. But it proved unfeasible, and he never bought the place. I guess now he's glad he didn't! That would have been about a $50,000 a year vacation home...

I'm hardly one to comment, as there but for the grace of God go I and <u>my</u> house, too. In fact, oddly enough, there — <u>because</u> of the plan of God for Cape Cod — will go I/we, unless we do something so expensive and so complicated as to arrange (with the Lesser Powers of this temporal sphere) to get out of its way, one day some iron dinosaur will show up in our yard, too!

HAS EVERYONE JOINED THE NAUSET LIGHT PRESERVATION SOCI-ETY?? (Be advised that Pam, its treasurer, keeps me apprised of all out-of-state donors... and "Mary kept all these things and pondered them in her heart" (Luke 2:19)... And, while we're flinging around Bible verses, how about 1 Thessalonians 5:5, which says, "But, dear brethren, you are not in the dark about these things... for you are all CHILDREN OF THE LIGHT." Ahem.)

The address of the Nauset Light Preservation Society is: PO Box 941, Eastham, MA 02651.

Any questions?

Love,

"Mother"

January 7, 1995: *Timothy (brother) sent me his latest poem (to/of/about his current inamorata), inviting comment, critique, and advice on when he should share it with her. It was fun to edit it and return it, even though I advised he NOT share it immediately. Impatient engineer that he is, he thinks if only he is more assiduous an admirer, the relationship will move along quicker toward the closer, longer-term one he'd like it to be. "BLOOM, dammit!" he's thinking as he pulls open the green sepals of what he wants to be a rose. Sigh. Do we ever learn this lesson except the hard way? I doubt we do.*

Maybe the best thing to come from Tim's poetry is that, itself: his own self-expression in a new and unusual medium. I'm both surprised and delighted that he's shown both interest and aptitude for it. And it's prompted me to do a new one, too: my first in years...

STORM AT NAUSET LIGHT

Just beyond the raw and ragged edge
Of this imposing cliff,
The ocean rests... for now.
Or perhaps it just takes smaller bites
Of the crumbling face –
For surely it is not appeased.
Of this now-normal noise,
This thin sound of receding surf,
I am distrustful
    And I cannot sleep

This must be how it is
To sleep with one
    – an alien by day –
Who rudely invades
    In the small dark hours
In piracy, brutality, with persistence
By rhymes and reasons unconnected
    to me, to mine, to anything I comprehend...
But whom I cannot leave.

Tonight the Beacon's soothing finger
Smooths the satin surface
Of the shimmering black sea
Just beyond the cliff's unraveling hem –
    Now six feet closer to where I lie
Than yesterday;
    Twenty feet nearer then when we wed
    (for better, for worse; for richer, for poorer).

But beneath this thin, smooth surface
Still churns the threatening rhythm
    of another front
Even as I try to close it out,
I feel it turning toward me again,
And the surly insistence
    of its burgeoning appetite,
Which only everything I have will sate.

The 1996 Relocation of Nauset Light and Oil House

13 February 1995 (Keeper's Log): *I came out last Thursday to check on things, scout out a few last facts for the book, and to attend Friday night's gala 10th anniversary celebration of the Eastham Forum, founded in my former house-watcher's kitchen. Quietly but firmly that group — now claiming 600 members — has affected and accomplished much in East-ham: open space preservation, zoning reform, additional traffic lights, and opposition to "govt-run-amok" in ways that would change the character of this little town forever for the worse.*

When I arrived, late, I was greeted by "Love Canal East" — an assem-blage of 55-gal. oil drums, yellow caution tape, a huge dirt pile sitting on a Poly tarp and a big hole excavated on the SE side of the Light, by its foun-dation. Evidently the Coast Guard removed a rusted-out oil tank that years ago supplied a backup generator, finding in the process that it had leaked into the surrounding soil. So, all work has stopped until the EPA, DEP, CE, and town Board of Health can file the "necessary" paperwork and cart away the excavated soil to Maine. (One presumes that some Maine soil, uncontaminated, will be brought in to replace it. Gee. Maybe next summer we'll have a wild potato harvest!)

I have seen the lovely site plan for the relocation of the Lighthouse, which is to serve as the discussion-basis with the National Seashore and town, from now on. It's nice to see my house and my Oil House on the plan too, almost as if it were certain I can go along. But, alas, I have no land over there yet, and although I (and my lawyer) are preparing our case for being entitled to some without having to forfeit ownership of the Keeper's House in some few years, it's far from a certainty... time will tell.

Join us in our campaign. Join the NLPS (address at the top of this page) please!!

April 17, 1995: The Monday after Easter (at the Light)... *Here am I at the Light again, one week after my last appearance here — a 24-hour* round-trip occasioned by the need to meet with the Coast Guard engineer and his toxic waste disposal subcontractor in my decimated driveway, following the 3-month-long extrication of the Coast Guard's ancient lighthouse fuel tank. Installed probably in the 1950s, about 3 ft below lawn level next to the Light tower, it had rusted and leaked kerosene or gasoline into the soil alongside and underneath the 6-ft thick tower foundation slab. As part of decommissioning a light, such details are tended to, often making a worse actual situation out of a potentially bad one. In this case, although the initial digging commenced Jan. 6, no one in the CG's Warwick, R.I. engineering office apparently knew that all but the tower-site and 10 feet of land around it was privately owned — or was it that the designers knew but didn't inform the executors of their design? I think that was it. For months I had been hounding the town officials involved, trying to get someone to tell me what was going on and when it would end, but no one returned my calls.

Through the Nauset Light Preservation Society President, I spoke in person to a "Warwickie" — Dan — and he finally tied all the wires together so an explanatory (and contrite) message could flow through them, just last Monday — and if I was willing to drive 3-½ hours down here, I could meet the perpetrators on the site and register my opinion about how I wanted my yard to look instead of like Love Canal East.

Friday, the twirly-mustachioed boss man and his crew spread me a new tan pea-gravel driveway (although they did not roll it as promised) — and I'm told that someday soon (in April) a load of loam and a covering of seed and straw or burlap will be put down, in an attempt to restore "Lou's lawn" to its important duty (if not verdant splendor) of holding down the dusty sandy soil around the lighthouse. Fine and good — if it ever happens.

On Wednesday at 10 a.m., a fellow from the Warwick engineering office will arrive to begin testing my well water for contaminants relating to the fuel leak. With the house foundation standing squarely between the tank site and my current well, I doubt we will find anything. But I'm concerned that presence of any contaminated soil ANYwhere on the property will *limit my future well-placement options, when this one runs dry. But then, I hope by that time I'm across the street — which brings me back to today's reason for being here again: THE OFFICIAL LEASE-SIGNING CERE-MONY BETWEEN THE COAST GUARD AND THE NAUSET LIGHT PRESERVATION SOCIETY, marking transfer of all but navigational-aid responsibility for the Nauset Light to the NLPS, beginning June 1 and continuing for 5 years. All the bigwigs were here (or their official represen-tatives): from the Coast Guard's 1ˢᵗ District HQ in Boston and the Aids to Navigation office at Station Woods Hole; from the Cape Cod National Seashore HQ in Wellfleet; from the NLPS; from the Cape Cod Times, the Cape Codder, and the Cape's Channel 11 TV... we even had a lighthouse buff from Birmingham, England among us!*

Best of all, my lawyer came out and we both met the brand-new CCNS Superintendent (on her first day on the job here) and agreed to meet offi-cially during the week of May 14ᵗʰ while I am here for the open houses on either end of Maritime Heritage week. At last, we can get this ball rolling toward resolution.

Captain B of CG Woods Hole suggested I look into transferring ownership to my youngest heir before that meeting in case an offer is made of lifetime tenancy (again). Not a bad idea... but can a 5-year-old own property in Massachusetts?

Following the official signing ceremony, remarks were offered by Rep. Studds' assistant, by Capt. B, Bill B our NLPS president, the CCNS Superintendent, and finally by me — in which I told all present that Miriam Rowell's spirit was among us, approving heartily of our efforts on behalf of this site which was so near and dear to her heart. Then we all came indoors — out of the bright sun and chill breeze — for a wondrous buffet of smoked seafood, salads, cheeses, dips, various breads and cakes, and pseudo-champagne punch. I had also set out the Bohland beacon model of my house, the Oil House and the Lighthouse, the album of historic photos, the guest log, and a copy of my manuscript, all of which netted attention and prompted interesting questions which I strove to answer with equanimity and optimism (as there was a full contingent of Park Service people milling about, not to mention several reporters).

By about 1:30 p.m. the place was mine again, and I felt as if we just launched a ship with only me aboard. As I told the reporters, "The interesting negotiations are about to begin," not bothering to explain that "interesting" comes from the ancient Chinese curse: "May you live forever in interesting times."

On May 17, I am due to give another of my grassroots pep talks about saving Nauset Light — this one to the Federated Church Women's group at Eastham's United Methodist Church. I intend to glean some interesting stories from my recently purchased book "Women Who Kept the Lights" (by Mary Louise Clifford) and to add to it my own update on the Nauset Light negotiations. I've written a new essay (from my old journals) called "Notes from the No-Name Nor'easter" — maybe that would be of interest to the ladies.

In any case, progress cannot be too speedy towards resolving this adventure: there's less than 10 feet left off the elbow of my driveway — evident at all times, now that the mashers have removed my brush pile during their hasty cleanup last week. It is most disconcerting how short the walk from the Light tower to the Cliff edge now is.

But at last we are on our way across the street. Aren't we?

Tuesday, April 18, 1995: *Last night I celebrated the end of a successful day and the beginning of a long-postponed good night's sleep by ingesting my first lobster of the season at the Lobster Pool with friend Joe L. Following dessert at Ben & Jerry's, home to my haven, where I opened wide the windows and — after talking with brother Tim awhile — sailed off into sweet sleep. I awoke at 12:30 thinking it was time to arise and function again, but soon savored my mistake and went back to Z-land until I could stay no longer. The pups and I got up at 6:20 and, after our bowlsful of breakfast, we went for a long walk on our beach, in a southerly direction. (We noted the continued presence of the dead pilot whale on the beach, though now considerably south of our original sighting.)*

Then we mailed off our 1994 income tax return (on the last possible day), bought a couple of local newspapers, and drove up to Wellfleet to Lecount Hollow to read them with a view of the ocean. I found myself quoted only briefly, thank God, on page A-3 in an otherwise nicely illustrated story about our celebration.

We couldn't pass up another beach walk, the pups and I, so we took another nice leisurely amble down that more northerly outer beach — a beautiful wide strand that I clearly remember from the late 50s – early 60s.

Mary on beach with Clipper and Polly.

The long shallow slope of the water-entry was irresistible to Polly, and Clipper soon followed — we were almost completely alone on that glorious stretch of beach for nearly an hour. As we left, though, it was clear we should hie our furry selves to a pond for a good rinse. So we hunted around Long Pond for a public access where the girls both rinsed and chilled themselves, glad to stop fetching the ball after just two plunges.

We visited Parkington's Mayo Beach Lightkeeper's cottage, noting the light-site now full of daffodils, then fetched some cold cuts and Portuguese rolls at Lema's Wellfleet grocery, and now we're home for lunch and to await the 2:00 p.m. arrival of the busload of kids from Vermont, who will tour the lighthouse under Pam's watchful eye. I'm loving this day, ripped from the wintery calendar of a New Hampshirean and enjoyed in the springlike sea air of Cape Cod. I'm not sure I want to go home tomorrow...

Tuesday, May 16, 1995: *At the Lighthouse. This afternoon at 3, my lawyer and I had our long-awaited meeting with the new Cape Cod National Seashore Superintendent and her land-use advisor. We met in that huge conference room, sitting opposite each other — we with our backs to an outside wall, they with theirs to their offices. Thankfully, the old boys of the old regime were not invited. (An excellent sign, thought I, that the new Superintendent needed no insulation from the public on this (she admitted) her "most complex and challenging project.")*

My lawyer began the discussion by presenting a thin glossy overview of the challenge as he sees it, from the point of view of a lawyer outside the Park with no preconceived notions, simply representing me, a person faced with the possibility of losing her house — and not just to erosion. I held my nit-picking tongue and watched the opposite side as they listened... And when the time was right (it seemed like <u>years</u>!) I threw in my points of emphasis: the wisdom of the Coast Guard back in 1957 forging a mutually beneficial long-term relationship with a private landowner — something we hope the Park Service can and will do again in handling this case; and the fact that this is a long-term commitment on the part of me and my family, not an attempt to "score" a plot of land, restore the market value of the buildings, then sell out.

Which segued nicely into my lawyer's unveiling of an idea I had agreed to on the ride over to Park HQ — that to demonstrate my commitment to the long-term maintenance of the structures, I would devise a trust for just that purpose, overseen and administered by members of a family board of trustees, for the next 75 years or until the next relocation is necessary, whichever comes first. That really caught their attention, and some notes were quickly taken: a good sign, said my lawyer. That I was willing to do this, above and beyond footing the relocation bill, seemed to be impressive.

I also offered my suggestions as to the future usefulness of the foundation (to support an observation platform like that of Marconi Beach and at

Skiff Hill), the patio (as a resting garden for those who've trekked up from the parking lot to (1) see the Lighthouse and to (2) take in the shoreline view), and the existing well and walkways. I even promised seed money for a matching grant to fund such a project outside the Park's thin budget: maybe the NLPS would consider it as a "coda" to their major effort to relocate the tower.

The Park Superintendent gave a speech about how she will be viewing all this, with much advice and input from others on her staff: she will necessarily be deciding on what is best from the Park's point of view in terms of stewardship of both funds and historic treasures for the greatest good of the greatest numbers. She said she'd never heard such a generous and comprehensive offer as mine.

The next step seems to be reaching a consensus with the NLPS and their Cape Cod Commission assistants on site evaluation and selection. (They are currently wasting time evaluating several other worthless and undesirable sites to satisfy the rules under which the Park labors.) Once identified, site evaluation begins before approval is granted. (Would I consider tagging along to some other site if one were chosen? You bet I would.)

I pointed out, however, that giving up something in the way of ownership of my house was not my only option (if they do not accept my proposal): I am still free to separate from the tower and move my house to another piece of land. "But that would be an eternal shame," I said, and gave them my "house without a tower" and "tower without a house" speeches.

When the historical remnant of the "limited tenancy" terms discussion was mentioned, I told them in no uncertain terms that I believed (as a person of age 51 who has twice nearly met her maker) such an offer would hardly be attractive if I were to consider the strong interests of my large and generally much younger family.

Likewise, when the "other management tools" were mentioned as needing to be applied in evaluating this case — namely (and she named it!) the disposition of the dune shacks in the Peaked Hill area of the Province Lands, I managed to contain my ire and say, after a moment's silence "You will never find in a limited-term tenant the will nor the means to do for these structures what I am proposing to continue in perpetuity to do..." which, of course, they readily acknowledged... and I could check another major point off my mental list of reasons why there is no better way than to let me continue here.

During the enumeration of all the Park resources that will be brought to bear in making this decision, the Superintendent's assistant mentioned historians and preservationists — and I made room to inject another sales point: that at the time of the relocation, I would be glad to entertain recommendations as to opportunities for restoration — e.g., the removal of the 1967 attached garage and the re-shingling of the exterior — perhaps even the reinstallation of those long-gone, wave-sawn verge boards.

I also made it a point to note the precedent set back in 1956 when the Coast Guard unmanned the Nauset Light, but with enough awareness to see the promise inherent in establishing a mutually beneficial constructive relationship with an individual civilian in order to preserve what the Coast Guard was unable financially to preserve itself: the essential character of the venerable Nauset Light Station. They signed over what they didn't need to someone who would care for it (at least) as well as they used to, and kept only what they could (had to) manage themselves: the Lighthouse and 10 feet around it, plus access over existing roadways. If federal agencies like these could find common ground and imaginative solutions such as private ownership and maintenance of what had once been federal property, it might behoove us to do likewise in these decades of fiscal restraint, in an effort to balance our budget.

I think that was our hour, and we parted amicably, agreeing to keep communication channels open during deliberations, not closed until all Park minds were made-up and closed forever.

OH — one other point made by my lawyer — or snuck in: he said maybe some things that are not possible for the Park to do, the town CAN do. So maybe the Park and I could give our swappable parcels to the town to reallocate as we hope they can be. The Park Service representatives both received that favorably — and (once I saw it wasn't intended as a hyper complexification joke) so did I! So, what I waited and sweated in anticipation of is at last over. And although I have no answer, my hope is renewed.

Thursday, May 18, 1995: This afternoon I will deliver my "7 IRONIES OF SAVING NAUSET LIGHT" speech to the women of the Eastham United Methodist Church, hoping all the while that they've either not already heard it or (horrors!) don't REMEMBER having heard it. This time, though, I can bring them up to date on my meeting with the new Park Superintendent, and can outline my proposal for them — which NLPS fundraiser Pam says sure can't hurt. In fact, says she, it is so comprehensive and so generous, that if the Park chooses another option they will look like fools.

So, I'm sitting here in the gray misty morning light (it's 8:37 a.m.) listening to the ocean roaring JUST outside my bedroom window, trying to reduce my proposal to a mnemonic — a sequence of memorable verbs, like "PRESERVE, PROTECT, and DEFEND." Best I can come up with is:

BEAR: the costs of relocation of the house, Oil House, garage
DONATE: my remaining 3.75 acres to the Park
PROVIDE: seed money to fund its future public use
FUND: perpetual maintenance and improvement to this house
RESTORE: the relocated buildings at relo-time, as funds last

The man who was a driving force behind the far-more-massive relocation project at Block Island Southeast Lighthouse, Dr. Jerry Abbott, is quoted as having said these memorable words:

"Nothing moves the imagination like a lighthouse. And nothing moves a lighthouse like imagination."

I could not have said it better myself. And I do believe (especially after having bounced my proposal off Pam and Joe) the Park has (as our CCNS Superintendent has said) never seen such a comprehensive... and IMAGINATIVE... proposal concerning an historical property within Park bound-

aries. Now it remains to be seen how hogtied by precedent they choose to be — or how willing they may be to setting a new precedent. Not for caving in to private interests but to setting a new, higher standard of cooperation with those of the Park inhabitants who are capable and willing to think more imaginatively than adversarially about preservation and land-use issues.

Thursday, 21 May 1995 (Keeper's Log): The log was signed on this date by guests (and close friends) Myric and Lois, and separately by their friend and traveling companion, Barbara Mugnai (Haskins), who included her address in Rhode Island and her phone number, and wrote simply this:

"Thanks for showing us my old home."

Mary's entry in the Guest Log, of the same date, explains:

Mrs. Haskins-Mugnai is the daughter of Allison "Ted" Haskins, the 8th Keeper of Nauset Light, from the time she was in first grade (at the old yellow, one-room schoolhouse across the street from the Salt Pond Visitor's Center) in 1932, until she was in the seventh grade at Nauset Elementary in 1938. Her father was posted here (her husband says) because the prior Keeper "was a slob" and "the place was a shambles, including the tower." Her father was a stickler for tidiness and cleanliness (so was her mother) and won the pennant for best-kept light station on the East Coast the very first year of his tour there. His contribution, which lives on today, is the first-floor bathroom. He had also fixed up the basement into an indoor gym/playroom for his kids and their cousins, including a half-court basketball area. Her mother and dad had a gorgeous rock garden on the street side. From here, he was posted to Woods Hole Coast Guard Station, which the kids (3 girls) liked better because "it wasn't so isolated as Nauset."

What a treat to listen as we toured the place and she told stories of how it was to live here — without electricity or neighbors or the National Park, or tourists!

My only regret was learning that her dad had been alive and keen-of-mind until 1988, and lived near Falmouth, I believe... I wish I had known... what a resource for my history of Nauset Light he would have been.

Cape Maritime Heritage week has come and gone. It began last weekend with a nor'easter testing the foul weather gear of the day's Lighthouse open-house attendees Cape-wide, who were then rewarded with a glorious Mother's Day to see the rest of the planned attractions. All the weekdays were rainouts (including Tuesday when my lawyer and I met with the new National Seashore Superintendent and formally proposed a land swap — my 3-3/4 acres including my 429 feet of Ocean Beach (to mean low water) for 1/3–1/2 acre across the street next to the relocated Light tower; and Thursday when I gave my "7 Ironies of Saving Nauset Light" speech again). But this weekend's open lighthouses were in glorious sunshine, much to the delight of my house guests, Dr. and Mrs. Myric Wood of Lebanon, New Hampshire. I will wend my way north tomorrow with renewed hope that the Park Service will grant me the necessary land-swap and all of us will be given a new 75-year period in which to enjoy this place before our grandkids have to go through all this again prior to the NEXT Nauset Light relocation.

And further, in connection with the same entry, Mary noted of Mrs. Haskins-Mugnai's travel companions (Myric and Lois):

The Wood family used to rent the last of the Three Sisters Lighthouses ("The Beacon") from Mrs. Harold Hall, who is now 94 and came to my lecture on Thursday, and shared many interesting stories about that small treasure, which now sits with its siblings in the piney woods ¼ mile up Cable Rd from its former home.

Thursday afternoon, May 28, 1995: *I am supposed to be in Lyme, New Hampshire, at this moment. Instead, I am sitting out on the patio by the Lighthouse tower, a cool breeze keeping me cool to the fringes of cold although I am bathed in brilliant sunlight. All about me spring is clipping along at double time to make up for last week's — and the week before's —*

damp cold obstructionism. It is as if God was keeping these most recent 4 days from us until they were just perfect, or at least until we could be more grateful.

I wish I could say I am still here because I had the sense of priorities to stay, after my assignments here were completed: my meeting with the Cape Cod National Seashore Superintendent, my lecture to the "Methodistes," my presence at a pair of open (Light) house weekends, and my providing a chance for friends Lois and Myric to return to the place where they used to bring their brood for summer vacation (or a part thereof).

I am in fact still here only because the very morning I was to leave (this brilliant one here, now) the Coast Guard's roving site engineer and his subcontractor showed up to put down loam and grass seed where Lou Rowell's lawn used to be, before the little fuel tank that leaked took four months to be removed from next to the Lighthouse.

But enough causation — here am I under a clear blue (too small a word) sky, a breeze in my face, birds bathing at my feet (almost), and the sound of the ocean with a descant of gleeful children's voices. Whatever my reason for being here, I am indeed blessed.

3 August 1995 (Keeper's Log): *The Nauset Light Preservation Society is having open (Light) houses here on Sundays in July and August, from 4–7 p.m., with my little garage at the south end of the property serving as the adjunct NLPS gift shop. Do visit and buy something. Also join up (for a mere $10) and help us raise the dough to move this set of antiques before Mother Nature does. We haven't had a big storm in almost three years (highly unusual) and now we are hearing that this year's hurricane season is predicted to be shaping up to be the worst in two decades. It doesn't take a rocket scientist to anticipate what might happen if we don't get this show across the road soon... and the only thing missing now is sufficient money. (NLPS has raised $90,000 in two years, but needs $225,000 or so for the move, and about $150,000 to endow a maintenance fund.) PLEASE HELP. (The storefront NLPS gift shop is located in the "Main St. Mercan-*

tile" shopping area on Rte. 6 (east side, south of the Lobster Pool) on Tues-days and Sundays from 10–1. Go see the $10,000 wall-hanging....

During the summer of 1995, our family turned its attention to our father, Benjamin K. Daubenspeck, who, at age 78, contracted a rare and particularly insidious cancer that worked its wiles fatally upon his system within a few short weeks of its discovery. Our dad learned of his cancer just after our annual July family reunion in Harrisburg, Pennsylvania, and passed away at the end of August at his home in Lyme, New Hampshire. The paralyzing impact of this event on our family was heightened by its suddenness, as Mary and all five brothers spent much of July and August rallying around in New Hampshire in support of our parents and of each other. In the after-math of our dad's passing, Mary devoted herself to further supporting our mother in Lyme, and found that during the next few months she was virtually unable to visit her beloved Keeper's House, save for a whirlwind visit in October to facilitate stocking of her newly written book in the local bookstores.

22 October 1995 (Keeper's Log): *"Mother" was here just for the weekend to get the new book (in living room, on trunk) stocked in a few local book shops, in addition to the Nauset Light Preservation Society shop at Main Street Mercantile, way back, open 9–1 Sundays. So far, I'm batting 1.000, and Compass Rose on Main Street in Orleans, Blue Heron Books in the Lemon Tree Pottery Shopping Center on 6A in Brewster, and Brewster Bookshop also on 6A have it in stock, if you can't wait to get a signed copy direct from me for $12.95 plus $3.50 S+H.*

We had a heck of a nor'easter yesterday — actually more of an "Easter," but that sounds so holy... The 40 MPH winds were pretty steady for about 12 hours, and the late rain was torrential at times. But (knock on drift-wood) this particular section of the cliff hasn't lost a major chunk since 1992, and last night just a few plants in the front row went over, into the orchestra pit. Please join the Nauset Light Preservation Society and help us get the dough to get this show across the road before it's too late: it's just

$10 for individuals, $20 for a family. Having stayed here, now, y'all do have a (pardon the pun) bit of an enlightened self-interest in the project.

There is truly no place like this home. I am so glad I resisted my dear father's admonitions to sell out before the big move became necessary. Bless his heart and soul, since August 28th, he's maybe had a chance to meet the former owner, my mentor Miriam Rowell, somewhere up there, and surely by now she's "converted" him to our preservationist way of thinking. (I hope it hasn't gone t'other way!)

In any case, let's enjoy it while we can — and work to extend that enjoyment to at least another couple of generations.

July 1, 1996: Full moon at the Lighthouse! 'Twas the night before... a critical meeting, one-on-one, of me and the Superintendent of the Cape Cod National Seashore to see if we can make some progress toward resolving our differences over the terms of the relocation of this glorious house across the street. She initiated the meeting, although I was about to — under the same minimal conditions: no staff on her side, no lawyer on mine. It is indeed an inspired thought, limited only by our mutual patience and imagination... or should I say our will to choose to not complexify what I have come to believe is a non-problem. And thereon is built what I hope to say in my opening remarks, given the opportunity.

- *There really is no problem here to be solved, if we will let it be so. My statement of intention (5/17/95), my mean financial support, and my reputation/history obviate the existence of a problem. I am only continuing the good work promised by the Rowell's to the Coast Guard in 1957. It is only CCNS's acquisitiveness, suspicion, and management fervor that has created the illusion of a problem between me and them.*
- *I have retreated over the past weeks from standing within this illusion of a problem and trying to accept concessions I am told will solve it. I now stand all the way back at the most pragmatic viewpoint born on the day the purchase was "closed." From this original vantage point, I see clearly that the Keeper's House and Oil House represent to me and my estate/heirs/family, first and foremost, a substantial asset useful to any and all of us potentially <u>forever</u> as, at least, collateral against unforeseen economic need or personal misfortune. When this asset is threatened with essential forfeiture to CCNS, the rational, optimal solution becomes relocation to private land elsewhere so as to reestablish and preserve that equity.*
- *It seems, from here, so obvious that people cede properties to parks when they are no longer able or willing to maintain them themselves. Parks accept such cessions as they can afford them. In this case, NEITHER situation exists, so my ceding the place to*

113

CCNS is not only imprudent but unnecessary — for either party! Pretending that it is necessary, and desirable, is only to break something that never needed fixing!

- *The essential question I am being asked by CCNS then becomes ridiculously silly: "How much are you willing to give up UNNECESSARILY, Ms. Daubenspeck, in order to have what you already have?" — Namely, the ways and means to keep the Nauset Light station intact for yourself and the public until the next relocation. The answer to the question is: NOT VERY MUCH, simply because it is so unnecessary!*

- *I seem to have spent the past two years in the middle of this muddle, trying to accommodate CCNS — to impress them with my sincerity. However, when I return to Square One — to the day I purchased the place for 1/3 of a million dollars — I see it simply, practically, newly: the only prudent course of action is to relocate elsewhere to land I own, in order to simply preserve the asset's value. This is hardly rocket science...*

- *The way for CCNS and me to resolve this is to simplify our view of it, to agree on our common <u>pro bono publico</u> goal, then bind ourselves to its accomplishment with a simple legal instrument clearly establishing the standards of compliance and the consequences of non-compliance... thereby allowing the working present to continue to function into the future, indefinitely.*

- *Let's not be motivated by some misguided, trumped-up populist worry that there is great pent-up demand for caring for the Keeper's House which is not being satisfied and will create problems for CCNS in the future. What demand there is, is being satisfied just fine, thank you, by my responsible sharing of the experience with (over 14 years) some 125 families, in exchange for maintenance help or coin of the realm. No one is requiring regular changes of management at the Highland Links Golf Course. My "conforming use" is no different.*

In any case, I expect no miracles from tomorrow's meeting. But I am shocked to find that the erosion has made the little Oil House today the most critically threatened structure on the patch — a huge semi-circle of land has disappeared between the elbow of the driveway and the next-door neighbor's house...

And on the path from the Lighthouse to the edge, where Soupy's and Hattie's and Derby's ashes were scattered in 1986, one can see sky and water just 10 feet in. By now most of those wonder-pups are afloat in the surf at the highest tides. ("Happiness is...")

I must sleep now. I hope I do not dream. I will be glad (no matter what is said or settled) tomorrow when this conference is passed.

Dear Miriam: stay with me. I'm doing what I'm sure you would do, as best I can. Love, Mary

The public interest in the Keeper's House at Nauset Light has forever been visual, and experiential only at arm's length. To destroy that as a result of some backstage bickering over who <u>owns</u> it would be more than a shame. It would be irresponsible of the one party here who WORKS for the public... and that is not I.

I have promised to see that 2/3 of Nauset Light (the Nauset Light Station) is relocated at my own considerable expense so that <u>all</u> of us can continue to appreciate it as it has always been. BUT ALTRUISM HAS LIMITS. And staying with the tower only to lose my house is not my only option. If CCNS can match the Daubenspeck's generosity and trust, we will <u>all</u> be enriched by the result — at no public expense. If not, we may all be forever impoverished by their smallness.

Thursday, 11 July 1996 (Keeper's Log):

Alas, it's time to head for the hills again, after sharing this place with family and friends for 11 days — a longer stretch than I've spent under Nauset's beam in a couple of years. Though the speed with which the cliff edge is advancing on the Lighthouse, the Keeper's House and the Oil House is astounding, progress in my negotiations with the Park people this week eases my anxiety, as did a couple of trips up to Truro to watch Highland Light "take the cure" instead of "the plunge!". If all goes well, we'll begin our trek across the street to relative safety in October, "God willing, and the 1996 hurricane season don't git us." The ultimate cost for this reprieve is surrender of the house to Park ownership, however, at some point — something I wish to avoid but can only hope to forestall. The past 11 days have been, then, a tutorial on enjoying what we have while we have it, because nothing lasts forever — Mother Nature and Uncle Sam are just too formidable. For now, however, I'll take with me the comforting thought that there are many nieces and nephews, brothers and sisters-in-law willing to care for this treasure as well as enjoy its many delights for as long as it is ours. God bless us, every one. Mary

23 August 1996 (Keeper's Log):

As Brother Tim wields the vacuum cleaner (!!!), I'll take a moment to gaze out the master bedroom window to the ocean, which is now just one row of valiant pine trees away from swallowing the driveway. All my "Sentinel Pines" at the elbow of the driveway are gone, over the edge and down to the beach. (Just five weeks ago, there were two on each side of that clearing.)

We came down with my pups but without Tim's kiddos, Heather and Ben — and it was strange being so irresponsible and un-parental/un-auntal for the past four stellar summer beach days. We cooked just one dinner (a luscious hours-fresh bluefish fillet) and ate out the rest of the nights. Lunches were always the same: we'd split a lobster "rollwich" from the Box Lunch on Route 6... slurp, drool, yum.

Wednesday, we conversed with the International Chimney Corp. President and Foreman (who are tucking Highland Light into its new site up in Truro) about our anticipated move — though I have not yet gotten the OK from the National Seashore powers-that-be that I am going along on the October retreat from the sea. (To say I am anxiously awaiting that is a colossal understatement.) I walked to the new light-site and house-site across the street with Hawkins Conrad, the Nauset Light Preservation

Society leader, and it seems fine, except for the unavoidably more public situation that results, even for our house. After the move, the Light will be walk-able-up-to at all times, though open just once a week or so. If we think the past 14 years "touroid" encounters were annoying at times, we likely have another think coming!

Thursday was the formal opening of the contractors' sealed bids for the job and there were just two — with International Chimney coming in lower on all counts, especially on my share of the move. Next week, the contract will doubtless be awarded to them, and we can all put on our relo-shoes and roll up our sleeves, load our cameras, liquidate our assets, and look forward to the big week in October! — Mary

Friday, August 30, 1996: *The other night I awoke at 4:00 in the morning with the question burning in my forehead: TELL ME AGAIN, MARY, WHY YOU ARE AGREEING TO GIVE UP THE KEEPER'S HOUSE — EVEN IN 60-SOME YEARS — TO THE FEDERAL GOVERNMENT?*

It was a question posed earlier in the day by the well services company representative "Shaun," at the house to replace the pump and holding tank — two major systems expenses I was hoping not to have to address before October's $80,000 move across the street. Shaun's questions were disturbingly basic, and in answering them, I sensed my own disbelief in the logic I have come to accept since my two-hour talk on July 2nd with the Cape Cod National Seashore Superintendent.

"Precedent?" howled Shaun. "WHAT precedent? No one else has such a property!" Suddenly I felt back at Square One, over on Shaun's skeptical side, questioning how I could have moved so far off my former staunch defense of the place from government seizure. Was there any reason other than the Superintendent's comfort that my Keeper's House should find itself upon this particular retreat/relocation in the ownership of the Park? How could this private owner's proposal to care for the place indefinitely at her and her family's own private expense not be accepted as a perfectly

adequate guarantee of cooperation in doing the Park's work with no taxpayer funding?

Sure, there is a set of privately owned properties in the park that are about to fall into the ocean. And sure, there is a set of historic properties — in Park or private ownership — that need maintenance and curators. But how many properties are in the overlap of those two sets? For it is only this common subset that enters into this fear-of-precedent consideration. I'll bet my Keeper's House stands alone in that space, the sole erosion-threatened privately owned historic structure CCNS has to consider. And <u>surely</u> the only one with an owner willing to accept a finite limit on her family's private tenure there.

Other questions I thought I had already answered to my own satisfaction followed close on the heels of this one, as I lay awake in the dark:

- *Why don't I just stay behind and hope to drive a better bargain in 10 years — perhaps with the Disney corporation, for big bucks?!!*
- *And why don't I keep looking for a relocation lot, to another privately owned parcel of land, bite the purchase price bullet, and preserve private ownership of this $350–500K asset?*
- *If I did go along on the big October relocation trip, and did not own the half-acre I was perched on, then who would be responsible for the well, the septic system, the access road — me or the Park? Who would maintain the actual property? Whose liability policy would pay for a trespassing tourist's broken leg?*

My head began to hurt. I was not just losing sleep, I was making myself crazy. I wondered if I should not, bright and early on Thursday morning, call the Superintendent and ask <u>her</u> this question: Tell me again why I have to <u>ever</u> give up my Keeper's House, a very valuable asset owned entirely by me, once I pay $80,000 to have it relocated? Instead, I called and left a message with her secretary that I was very anxious, now that the contract had been let, to know if I were to be included in next month's relocation. I was told she would be in touch as soon as anything was resolved.

And this morning I received such a call, at 9:00-ish...

Although no decision on my proposal has officially been made, the Park Superintendent reports it looks very much like the most I can hope for is life tenancy or twenty-five years (whichever is longer?), if I choose to lease a half-acre of Park land to which to relocate my house, at my expense. And an "equity payment" to compensate me somewhat for my relocation costs looks iffy at best: "As you know," she said, "there *is* no money in Washington."

In addition she referred to my two-page commentary on the proposed plot plan as "a bit of a cold slap in the face," reacquainting her with the myriad potential problems that go along with a private homeowner on that newly public-accessible site across the street; this makes NPS all the more certain that the shortest-term deal is the better.

I mentioned I had heard that the Park Service favors either 99-year or 49-year land lease agreements, but she acknowledged hearing only of 10-year agricultural land lease arrangements in her previous Fredericksburg, VA, experience [SLAM!].

I must say, I concluded, I am extremely disappointed that a group of small-minded, short-sighted i-dotters and t-crossers in the bowels of the NPS legal, Accounting, and Lands-office departments seem to be disallowing an imaginative, cooperative agreement of the very sort which CCNS's brand-new three-year, million-dollar General Management plan seems to be pledging heart-felt allegiance to...

I said to her (I confess, tearfully) that my family will be convening this weekend for a memorial celebration for my dear father, and we would all discuss this. However, it seemed on the face of it, that we would want to now look at other options — which makes me very, very sad.

No one would doubt my motives from the book I wrote arguing for the retention of the three historic structures together at almost all costs, said I.

But neither would anyone be unsympathetic with my disappointment and with our need to fully investigate other options to preserve our investment and our lasting love for this house of ours. The Superintendent agreed, and said now that the General Management plan was off the front burner, the resolution of this problem was _on_ it. I left her my e-mail address which she said she would confirm the correctness of today, and that I would hear from her as soon as possible.

I did allow that we may have more time to resolve this, as even though I dearly wish to avail myself of the economies of timing inherent in going along on the October relocation of the lighthouse and Oil House, the ocean is not yet in my basement. Good, said she, because a land swap would take a year to finalize. My hopes soared: A LAND SWAP? Did she say A LAND SWAP? I thought that was not even on the table! Well, a straight land swap _is_ off the table — she's talking about a land swap coincident with a 25-year or lifetime tenancy agreement. Oh.

Pam says, "Hey: you can always relocate south on the property, down to where the boathouse is (there's at some point to be a closing of Nauset Light Beach Rd, but the seashore parking lot is always going to be there...)." Although I pooh-poohed that idea when she brought it up, that was yesterday, when I still believed I could get 60 years across the street! This is today, when I no longer believe that's possible! Why NOT move south — it's still a goodly distance from the cliff edge — maybe 20 years' worth! Hmm.

So who knows what will happen? Maybe I should buttonhole Gerry Studds' dynamic and involved aide, and tell him the bottom's falling out of the perfect resolution. But what could he do? Fact is, unless I choose to move my house farther away than 1/4 mile, no one may even care that the three National Register-listed structures aren't exactly right next to each other on the same plot of land. In fact, when the road is closed, who's to say they aren't?

And if I am to relocate my house to my own property why not do it next month when I can still take advantage of the economies of scale of the big move: namely, not having to absorb any of the "mobilization costs," (though maybe having to absorb all of the old-foundation-site-reclamation costs... And what are those? I'll have to ask...)

And... how should I view the prospect of my existing land being ripped up to make a roadway via which the Lighthouse and Oil House can be relocated across the street, but not my house? As long as I remain a resident on this plot of fragile land, I should do all I can to preserve its integrity, as it is all that stands between me and the sea! Now, in this new stay-behind scenario, I won't want to have the Light and Oil House moved except via the existing rights of way: namely, the driveway. Hmm x 2.

Rick L thinks moving to the boathouse site has always been a neat idea, and not just because it means not having to cede my house to the feds: it lengthens the house's life, improves its foundation, restores some equity, preserves the relative proximity of the three National Register structures, and preserves future generation's options: i.e. sale, a better relocation deal next time it's threatened, or retention for their own enjoyment.

He advises me to apply for a permit to cover a same-site move ASAP and to cash in all the goodwill chits I can in doing so: telling everyone about my donation of the Oil House and allowing a through-site lighthouse move (which, incidentally could be done via the driveway, using narrower axles and additional cribbing).

He says I'll get a good new foundation, new systems, new windows, and he could rig me a nice short-throw driveway and garage right off the street at the corner of the property. (He'd use the existing well.)

2 September 1996 (Keeper's Log) (excerpt from friend and guest, Susan L):

Dear Mary — Wow, what an experience! ... We awoke on Sunday to huge slate-colored clouds and the threat of Edouard the hurricane coming upon us that evening. I stopped at the Eastham police station, and they thought the storm was heading right for us with winds up to 100–115 mph. Wow!

So, we bought candles, got out all the flashlights, put out a change of clothes, packed our bags, and parked our cars at the end of the driveway in case we had to evacuate! The rain started around 7:00 p.m. and by 11:00 p.m. the wind was up to 40 mph. As we listened to the radio (electricity still on) the reports were changing and saying the hurricane was heading slightly east which meant we might just get grazed instead of a direct hit.

Before going to bed, we prayed that God would keep us safe and watch over and protect this house, the Lighthouse and all the people here on the Cape.

4:30 a.m. — are we crazy!??! We are all staying upstairs, and the wind is shaking the timbers! You can feel which way the wind is blowing and pushing the house. She seems to take each blow with strength and dignity like a grand lady.

By daybreak, our fears subsided, and we welcomed the light. We ventured outside to see that some more of the cliff was gone behind the Oil House, a few limbs down, bushes pushed over, and some roof tiles scattered about. I called the radio station WQRC 99.9 FM to inform them that we made it through the storm.

Thursday, October 17, 1996: *At Nauset Light. Friday night, when I arrived from New Hampshire at about 6:45 p.m., I noticed way down at the crest of the hill near the Coast Guard Station that there was no blink of the Light — my accustomed first welcome. I hoped the Coastie's ANT team hadn't already pulled its plug before I could get in my last night with my night light! At the stop sign at the Seashore parking lot, though, I could see the problem: although still shining, the big aerobeacon was binding in mid-rotation, stuck this time with the red lens facing me (SW) and the white one northeast out to sea. Strange. First time I'd ever seen it do this trick. By the time I had pulled up to the tower, however it was freely rotating again, and seemed fine until 9:30 that night, when the pups and Kitty and I were startled at the arrival outside our master bedroom window of a car. I flipped out my reading light and crept to the window. Peering out, I saw Hawk Conrad, the NLPS President staring up at the beacon in disbelief. "Someone told me the light was stuck," he said. "I sure* *hope it's not gonna turn itself off! Heck, that's supposed to be my big moment tomorrow at the (groundbreaking/decommissioning) ceremony: flipping the switch."*

By then, however, we were able to deduce/determine that it was a motor overheating problem — when the rotation mechanism bound up (who knows exactly why), the beacon's motor would overheat and shut down. When it had cooled sufficiently, it would resume normal operation till it got stuck again. That's the physics of it. But I think it's a more complex happening than can be explained by mere mechanics. I think this venerable tower, nearly 120 years in service, first at Chatham and for the past 73 years here in my yard, knows what is about to happen because it — unlike us — has witnessed it all before. In a marvelously simple way it was telling all us engineers and surveyors, constructors and movers, functionaries and fundraisers that we are the worker bees, not the queen or the hive.

Saturday's ceremony was held in my Keeper's House backyard filled with 300+ folks including bigwigs and the press, kids, dogs, and lighthouse lovers, under clear blue skies, with a huge American flag billowing out from the porch waving at the blue-green sea that has triumphed once again over the best laid plans of a similar group gathered here, no doubt, in 1923 when the last light-retreat from the ever encroaching cliff edge commenced.

Just a single-row scrim of pines now stands at the cliff top between the Keeper's house and Lighthouse and the ocean. The sun glinting off the water made us all squint as Hawkins Conrad shared some very gracious prepared remarks, spreading sincere thanks around to all who enabled this to be not just a decommissioning, but the start of a relocation leading to a relighting, sometime before Christmas, when Nauset Light will begin its new life as a privately maintained aid to navigation, perhaps about 75 years from the need for yet a third retreat.

That day I also handed Hawkins the signed transfer document for the Oil House, which my lawyer had brought along — it is now about 20 feet from its cliff edge and is thus the most imperiled of the three National Register-listed structures. I did not want its future safety precluded by the tangled negotiations I and the National Seashore appear to be stalled in. Saving it by disowning it was just the right and necessary thing for me to do. I do know, however that it will cost something to relocate it, and although I would gladly have borne that cost myself, I can't say I was disappointed when told that the NLPS would foot that bill without second thought or ill feeling.

Oil House donated by Mary Daubenspeck to CCNS for preservation in 1996 during Light relocation.

Although useless to me, I loved owning and protecting that beautiful little brick house-let, and I remember in 1982 fantasizing (as once did Miriam) that if only the odor of flammable lamp fuel could be removed from its brick floor and walls, and a window installed — maybe even a skylight — it would make a neat little annex, for sleeping — or as a potting shed.

Down at the boathouse, Pam did a land-office business before, during, and after the ceremonies, taking in some $4K between ten and four p.m.

Mary welcomed the Nauset Light Preservation Society (NLPS) to freely use her boathouse for the sale of Lighthouse memorabilia for the purpose of funding the Lighthouse relocation.

The Moving Moment of the Day, however, was when at the end of the ceremony, Captain Duncan told Electricians Mate First Class (E-6) Robert L (nephew Benny's buddy) — "Extinguish the light." And the switch was flipped for the final time at this historic site — the land that has been the Nauset Light station since 1838, for 158 years. It evoked an audible sigh from those gathered, as if we all were united for a moment in the almost tangible, and clearly audible, emotional impact of what we were doing.

Saturday morning I had awakened well before dawn and stood at the Keeper's bedroom window for a long time, taking in the last of these beacon-lit colors: the deep cobalt blue of the sky: Venus shining so brightly above the eastern horizon that it left a shimmering trail on the calm ocean surface; the blackness of the pine tops turned momentarily dark, dark green as the beacon passed above them... I was deeply moved to think I would not witness this comfortingly familiar sight again for a long time — months perhaps, and possibly never again. It was as if a friend were expiring just outside this window, and I helpless to reverse the course of that unfortunate event.

Saturday night, however, was even more somber, as I went to bed with no protective beacon regularly renewing its pattern on my bedroom walls, the black, black night oppressive in its unrelieved opacity. The greater number of visible stars in the sky was small compensation to me — I see that all the time in the mountains of New Hampshire. I felt like an older child finally deprived of her night-light, knowing it was "for my own good" but hating the imposed unfamiliarity it brought to my latent sense of nighttime vulnerability. I was glad to have Clipper, Polly, and even Kitty Mew snuggled close beside me.

Monday and Tuesday were chilly days, with northeast winds whipping up a surf-incursion angling toward us from the same direction as in the No-Name Nor'easter of just six years ago, when Clipper and Mew and I lived here, between houses, as it were. Sunday and Monday we had been serenaded (NOT!) by the sounds of chainsaws and a chipping machine across the street, as the landscaping subcontractor Shawn of Truro, cleared a 25-foot swath into the relocation site, running from just across my driveway southeast to the top of the knoll across from my boathouse.

On the third day, Tuesday, they arrived on my north property line to cut a similar gash in the woods that separate me from the next-door neighbor's property. I told them what I had said to International Chimney Company's Site Supervisor two days earlier, that I hoped they'd take no more trees out than necessary because each of them around the Oil House were so loved they had names. ("Merle" had wryly responded, "Well say goodbye to Fred and George there, 'cause they'll be the first to go.")

The subcontractor was sympathetic but forced to obey orders, taking every tree back to — and including — the orange-blazed ones, but leaving "Sally" the slim, fragile, lovely cedar by the Oil House's west wall. I know it too will have to go even though it was left unblazed, but at least it can enjoy life for another few days until the mistake is discovered and corrected.

The clearing is devastatingly broad — necessary, I know, but brutally extensive, and it leaves behind astonishingly small piles of chips that once were 40-year-old pines, oaks, and cedars, not to mention the varied understory of bayberry, beach plum, juniper, and cherry. The smell of the arborage (vegetage?) is still emanating from the battlefield, days after the machines' temporary victory.

A husband-wife team of core sample drillers was here yesterday sampling the soil to 25 feet from the Light and on the near and far sides of the Oil House to determine its compactibility under the weight of the heavy moving machinery, I presumed. (But when I asked Mel up at Highland Light yesterday, he said it was only to get numbers to enter into forms required by the engineering firm subcontracted by the government. "It's not as if this soil were just put here yesterday," he said. "It's had thousands of years to compact. Our machinery will compact it further only about 1/4 inch.")

Today a surveyor team came to mark out the exact center of the access road clearing across the street, so I suppose it's just a matter of days before the bulldozers arrive and gouge out the permanent base for that "scar of wonder, scar of light."

Oh, yes. Yesterday, the Park Superintendent's assistant introduced me to the landscaping designer for the relo site and said she was mailing to me a revised site plan, saying, "You'll notice we've incorporated some of the changes your comments prompted." I had a momentary flashback to the Superintendent's recent remark, "Your extensive comments, frankly, made us question whether you can be happy in the now more visible situation the relocation of your house would put you in." And I was ever-so-slightly tempted to say something crow-like, claiming influence upon the process and credit for common sense, but I refrained. (Good girl, Mary. You may have an extra dessert tonight!)

I had to miss my Humane Society board meeting in New Hampshire last night (with much advanced notice, I might add), and we'll stay till Saturday to see what's next. If I am to follow this process for a possible book-addition chapter, I should be here as much as I can for the next few weeks — not only to wait for Mark F of Congressman Studds' office to work his magic — but to document this construction process, unlike the last relo which left no written record at all, and that was just 73 years ago.

I will return as soon as I can and stay for as long as I can. This is what I've been waiting for, for almost 15 years! And it's clearly a once-in-a-lifetime opportunity.

Monday, October 28, 1996: *At the Light. Valerie, Mike of ICC (a southern cowboy looking guy), and Bob of ICC, are out in the Light tower sketching in their lines for tomorrow's first real act of the long-awaited play called — what? "The Light Moveth? Goeth?" Mike wielded the chalk (three seagulls on the floor to start with), Bob called out the calculated distances from the mini-first step of the spiral stairway, and Valerie said, "Sounds good to me." And tomorrow the diamond blade circular saw will rip the center out of the Light tower's floor, exposing the dirt below (and the bones of an assistant keeper maybe!). The crew says I may watch as long as I bring coffee.*

I drove down in spitting rain and arrived to unload in steady showers, but Hawk says tomorrow is to be better: merely "cloudy." But after the showers came a real treat: an ocean-rooted double rainbow, as the sun burst through the western edge of the dome of cumuli and finished the dull day with a technicolor light show. I stood at the elbow of the driveway, 4 feet from the cliff edge, and silently applauded the show. A few dozen seagulls flew out over the leaden water in the middle distance, back and forth, in and out of the rainbow light which was reflected broadly on the water surface. As the sun sank from sight, the sky above turned blue in diffraction and the ominous lower clouds evolved a docile pink. It was a good sign, I think...

The little Oil House stands bare in the surgical field that was its former hiding place. Almost all the trees near it have disappeared, though Merle has left some to its right, maintaining a row to drop one by one over the edge in the future. The Oil House steps are gone and the string that held its door shut blows in the breeze. But it really looks proud and square and every bit the preserved treasure that it is. I am glad to have been entrusted with it for 15 years and it feels strange to accept from Hawk a letter of appreciation from the Nauset Light Preservation Society for my donation of it 10 days ago. I'll continue to think of it probably in the same way as I have Harriet's and Clipper's puppies when they left my care.

There are the end-of-the-day sounds of the backhoe as it finishes the excavation of the new foundation octagon for the Lighthouse... this one to be solid. It's dark as I write this, but no matter: Valerie says the truck with the forms will come tomorrow, and Hawk says he's made the decision to pour concrete tomorrow no matter what. He's gotten the approval of all the abutters over there to relinquish their claim to owning to the centerline of the "paper roads" that still exist in theory over there in the woods — vestiges of a God-awfully misguided pre-Seashore plan — to divide up this whole shorefront into six or eight house blocks of 0.2 acre lots, with addresses like 3rd Ave. and 2nd St.

The last approval came from the elderly lawyer brother of a 92-year-old woman in a Connecticut nursing home, who said, grudgingly, "That lighthouse keeps getting closer and closer to us." God bless Hawkins Conrad and his army service, which his wife says was concentrated in the area and art of negotiation and compromise. NLPS was fortunate to have him on deck when Bill Burt left the post.

Happy to be here for a few days, to watch the event unfold, the staging of this play, but I'm also sad to see all the changes in the landscape. Nothing about this relocation is surgically pristine and minimally invasive, though it is clear that some effort is being made to be less brutal than possible. Would that we could have borrowed from Star Trek's armamentarium and just BEAMED the buildings across the street.

"THERE IS SO MUCH YOU THINK THAT ISN'T NEEDFUL TO SAY"

— *Kate Walker (1842–1931), Keeper of New York Harbor's Robbins Reef Lighthouse from 1886 to 1919*

Tuesday, October 29, 1996: *As I sit here in the Keeper's bedroom, at sunrise, with the sand-blasted east windows diffusing the liquid golden heat that enters and warms us, I think... And I say... What it seems to come* *down to, vis a vis me and the Seashore, is making and justifying a defensible exception for my family and our ownership of this historic treasure of a house. The latest round in the ongoing battle between the long-term leaseholders of private dwellings within the Park and the Seashore, their landlord who is calling in their leases, indicates the Park will be making distinctions for "hardship cases" — e.g., the very elderly, the infirm, folks with no other place to go, or no money to get there. And these are cases of exception to binding legal agreements, not just custom or Park policy.*

So... if exceptions can be risked and made to existing legal documents, decided cases involving relatively ordinary non-historic structures, then I would think surely, they can be made where there is no basis for public objection; where this private homeowner's huge capital investment and demonstrated faithful sharing stewardship for 15 years in an irreplaceable one-of-a-kind National Register-listed house — is indisputable.

To limit my family's private stewardship of this Keeper's house because there are others who might want to try their hand at it seems arbitrary and sycophantic. Where were those people in 1981 when the place was for sale? Where have they been ever since, when others have asked to spend responsibility-free weeks here and, when they have shown the required good faith, have been permitted to do so? The status quo here is serving the structures and the Seashore's best interests — why upset that and "fix" what ain't "broke"? I recall what Mark F first said, if the Park wants the structure to do with what <u>they</u> want, then let them make the present rightful legal lawful owner an offer to BUY it — an offer which I, as any other citizen, may accept or refuse, and if refusing, may move my house elsewhere.

I will make myself into anything (curator, concessioner, etc.) I have to in order to keep my house in my family's rightful private ownership. Anything, that is, but a fool.

The promised "cloudy" never materialized, as today's sun is potentially summertime warm and all we have to moan about is the 30-knot north wind which keeps us bundled up. At 7:15 a.m. the diamond circular saw (with its three-foot diameter blade) was set in place inside the tower and its compressor started up. Within minutes it was moving imperceptibly along its track, slicing three parallel cuts through the 8-inch-thick floor that spans the four-foot-deep footing (the octagonal base we all thought was solid... "we" being the sidewalk superintendents).

After lunch, the crosswise cut(s) were begun, "slicing and dicing" according to Bob. Valerie said another ICC crew was down in Marion, MA, setting out to refurbish the Bird Island Light a mile offshore — in hardly balmy conditions. Our section of the ocean is diagonally grooved in white capped north-northeasterly waves that look at least three feet high to me (the shorewalk superintendent).

Across the street, the power shovel takes the circular tower foundation excavation down another 2 ft. – 4 ft., like the Oil House's neat square one is. Forms will be in by day's end and concrete poured tomorrow.

Chuck K, who owns one of the summer cottages back in across the street, called and said he's the news director for Boston's Channel 5 and when the Light is actually up and moving, he wants to do an interview with me. "Fine," said I, wondering if by then I will still be able to keep a civil tongue in my head.

It's 10 minutes of 5, and as the sun sets, the temperature really drops, but the generator's diesel engine — and now the jackhammer and power chisel it is driving — is still filling the yard with noise, as the first chunk of concrete tower floor is being removed, not neatly in one long rectangular slab, but, in a thousand and one ragged stone-size chunks. It is surely resisting its demise, and it makes me even more impressed with how strongly and silently it has done its thankless task here since 1923. It is not going away quietly. I recall reading in the bid presentation that jackham-mers would not be used — the diamond-blade saws would be instead — in order to spare the tower the vibrational assault on its wall's integrity. OK, that was then. This, however, is now...

No concrete was poured today. Instead, the foundation holes were finished and the reference stakes imposed within them — with some unplanned readjustment for their being imposed with a significantly large offset, which all hoped was uniformly erroneous. And, by midafternoon, the Brewster concrete subcontractor still was not here with his forms, though the offset problem filled in nicely in his unexplained absence.

In today's Cape Cod Times, I found a quote by former Massachusetts U.S. Senator Leverett Saltonstall, one of the original sponsors of the bill that created the Cape Cod National Seashore in 1961:

> "The most important and complicated problem before us is to preserve the scenic and historic features of Cape Cod without injuring or unduly restricting the towns and individual citizens directly connected."

The quote lay within an article reporting that the Park Superintendent has gone against the recommendation of (advice of) federal attorneys and approved a land-swap with Provincetown to allow them to actually own their own dump... Perhaps if she gets used to the applause she got at last night's special town meeting for being so reasonably accommodating, she might begin to feel more inclined to be so in my case. Also perhaps not.

A defensible departure from General Policy = A Worthy Goal...

Wednesday night, October 30, 1996: Today I finally met my next-door neighbors, Jane and her husband Ed. I think they're my age or a year or two younger, and her parents have lived here since the early '60s and are, alas, both no longer with us. Their little cottage is about to be moved back from the cliff edge for the third time, so this will be its last hurrah at this site. They have not been to the Keeper's House since Miriam sold it to me. (Their fondest visit there was on their honeymoon when Lou and Miriam had them over for two hours of martinis and then a dinner of "Steak à la moutarde" that burned their taste buds for several days.) So tomorrow they'll mosey over for the tour. As I was leaving, they offered me their basement in which to store stuff from mine, if and when the house gets moved. It's a fine and spacious and wholly vacant space! What luck! Now all I need is a contents-relocation squad...

It rained off and on today — sometimes hard — so the concrete forms guy never showed up across the street. But "my guys," Bob and Mike, after a couple more hours with the jackhammer and chisel, finally got the tower floor to give up its first of two concrete slabs — it was raised up and hauled out (by Bobcat) like a pulled tooth, around noon. The second slab came out much easier, with nice smooth diamond-saw-blade polished edges, just as nice as you please. The guys have no idea why there was a difference between them, but both were over a foot thick, contrary to the plans the Coast Guard had provided them, which showed the floor to be just 8" to fill-dirt. Even the two test drillings hadn't prepared them for 12" plus.

This afternoon, as Mike shoveled fill out to a depth of about 2 feet in the tower, Bob busted up the Oil House's floor and began shoveling fill out of it also. (I managed to salvage one intact brick souvenir.) Tomorrow's weather looks good — clear and 55°F to 60° — so I'm sure there will be lots of progress made on both sides of the street. And, speaking of progress...

The assistant to the Superintendent at CCNS sent over a copy of the revised landscaping and road and trail placement plan for the relocation site and again made the point of saying it incorporates some of the changes I suggested a couple months ago. But there is no news to report on my front, and her boss is out of town for the week. No news is not good news. It's not bad news either — it's just annoying.

This evening I spent an hour completing the 15-year follow-up question-naire from Harvard's School of Public Health that proposes to extend the findings of the 1981 survey I participated in. Its angle is the connection between participating in athletics in college — the Seven Sisters schools for the most part — and health (particularly vis a vis cancer and reproductive history) 15 and now 30 years postgrad. Just completing the review called for by the questionnaire restored my perspective somewhat, on this "CCNS vs moi" episode in my really long and varied life so far. No matter how this mystery unfolds, I am far luckier than I daily consider, in having good health, a good brain that — if it doesn't solve <u>this</u> knotty problem will be just as ready and able to tackle another someday. I guess what I am saying is that the reflection on my mortality which the questionnaire's inquiries provided made me see that I am bigger than this conflict and not defined by it. And if it doesn't end up going my way after I've given it my best shot — now and perhaps in a couple of years when the ocean is at my doorstep — then fine. I'll move on to something else. It will not be a life-defining defeat. Fortunately. Blessedly. But it will, at some point, be OVER. Fortunately. _Very_ blessedly.

Thursday evening, October 31, 1996: All the digging here at Nauset Light has been moving toward a hopeful end. The footings were created across the street: an octagon for the tower and a square for the Oil House, which, until now, has stood on dirt. Its interior floor was a course of brick set into a ¾-inch slab of cement — sans aggregate — with mortar poured around the edges to link it to the double-course-thick walls. For its next 100 years, it merits a nice level concrete footer framed today with fresh, unused, clean white lumber. Nothing but the best for my pal.

One of the testing company guys asked how long this new site would last compared to the old one. We said at about the same time — somewhere between 70 and 100 years, but there was no way to calculate a reliable estimate. Then one of the "concrete" crew said, "Whatever it is, we won't know about it." Then, after a moment's thought, he added, "It's a good thing we're not still living in Biblical times, because if I were like Moses, I'd have to do this about 4-½ more times." The same guy later made another amusing remark. I asked him as he was "floating out" the last nice smooth surface of the Oil House footer, "Are you ever tempted to leave your mark in the concrete, like tradesmen and craftsmen used to?" "No," he replied, "First of all, it would never be seen — and secondly, the only way it _would_ be seen is when the footer separated from the foundation, and since that would mean I did it wrong, I'd rather they not know what 'craftsman' screwed it up!"

By day's end, I really felt as if we had really moved this project forward, setting down something new and, well, "concrete," at the new site. The Oil House was framed at the corners with nice heavy corner-guards and the first big cable-and-turnbuckle assembly binding the corners tightly together was in place. Bob and Mike's work for tomorrow was laid out:

excavating a six-foot-deep hole in the exposed dirt in the center of the tower and starting the external, west-side excavation where the "cross steel" H-beams will be threaded through diagonally opposite faces of the octagonal foundation walls.

The Oil House sits open tonight, as poor Bob hit the door "just right" while working in there this morning, such that the lower two panels just shattered and the bottom stile fell out in a couple of pieces. I told him it had been "on the verge" for quite a while, having been tied shut for years because the bottom stile wouldn't clear the seal. ICC will probably need to build a new door, but I feel as if I might perhaps put some sort of contribution into that kitty.

Speaking of whom, without its floor, the Oil House is just a big, tall, brick box filled with sand: a giant historic, antique kitty litter box. If it weren't still redolent of kerosene fumes, I'd let Kitty Mew try it out.

Ed and Jane came over for cocktails and a house tour tonight, as did Valerie and Mike from the crew, whom I had promised a LAND HO! fish and chips feast. We had a fine time visiting and listening to structure-moving and helicopter-test-piloting stories. When they left, they said they'd like to talk to me tomorrow about a connection they've got with someone with the New York Times who may be interested in doing a human-interest piece about my predicament (and they left me a key to their basement, so I can store anything I want to from my cellar and basement therein, should I be informed I can go along on this relocation adventure... I SURE WISH WE COULD HAVE POURED A THIRD FOOTING TODAY).

I've just learned that the official re-lighting of Highland Light is scheduled for Sunday at 5:30, with the speeches at 5. U.S. Senator Bob Kerry will likely be there, as may his opponent, Governor Weld, and Congressman Gerry Studds... and maybe even Ted Kennedy. So, it would appear that I should not turn down my invitation, despite the fact that it will mean having to miss — or reschedule — Andy's birthday dinner scheduled for Sunday — which information will be greeted like a grenade by Mom when

I tell her. Oh dear, and oh well... <u>This</u> is what I must do now. There is simply nothing more important to me than seizing every opportunity to make this Keeper's House relocation happen without having to forfeit it. This is my vocation. I cannot compromise it.

Saturday, November 2, 1996: *The new trail proposed by CCNS as a path to the new Light site from the Seashore's parking lot makes a reasonable bend to avoid the corner of my land they had originally proposed running it over, and the crew put up a new post-and-rail fence section to obstruct the vestiges of a path into the south section just this side of the boathouse. It was all so obvious that that was where the Park's trail ought to go, it just makes me wonder why they even considered putting any of it on my land in the first place, when they did earlier.*

———————

I just had a chat with Rick — head of International Chimney — about what he would advise me to do with tomorrow's opportunity — i.e., assemblage of politicians at the Highland Light relighting. I thought of asking him to say to one or two of them that it would be real nice if someone at the Park would make a decision so my house could be included on this move, while everyone and all the equipment necessary was on site. I was just stunned by his reply: "I'm afraid we've already passed the point of being able to move your house this time," he said. "I told Hawkins that about a week ago."

It involves excavation equipment logistics (involving the stuff left on Wednesday morning) and concrete cure rates — i.e., the Keeper's House foundation had to be poured with the other two or it wouldn't be cured in time to receive the house.

"You mean I'm now left to the mercies of some local mover if and when the Park makes a decision I can accept?" I asked.

"Oh no," he said, "I can still come within a reasonable range of the bid price and use the outfit we worked with on the Providence job. They've got the truck and we could do this next spring."

I think he said the Providence guy uses Peter Friesen's system (the hydraulic-jacked dolly truck). He continued: "I think your job is just to sit tight right here and wait for them to make the move happen. The longer you do, the more they'll want the house to be over there with the tower." And the more people see that it's not and hear my story about <u>why</u> it's not... which I guess I am about ready to start trumpeting from the housetops, I am so angry about it.

(And why am I only now finding out about this critical bit of info? That I have now officially missed the boat? Why, all my life, have I been the last to know this kind of bad news — it seems that people are always reluctant to tell me bad news. Is it just <u>me</u>? Or do they do this with everyone else they deal with too?)

Virgil and his crew (Archie the tower-climber and John the fullback) arrived this morning in their small sporty maroon truck, all the way from Missouri — part of Expert House Movers' Midwest branch office. Seems like the wrong word to use — "office" — when it seems that these guys spend their lives on far-flung jobs all over this country, and outside it too. (Mike was kind enough to share with me his portable picture file of snap-shots, which runs the gamut of jobs from an industrial chimney in State College, PA, to the mammoth Southeast Light on Block Island, to the entire town of Rhine, which was moved up into the nearby hills after two horren-dous floods.)

The Missourians set about framing the Light tower in scaffolding reminis-cent of Highland's gallery deck, and to repair a couple of cracked and sprung deck brackets — something that could be dangerous during a move of this sort. (Imagine the "handsome gentleman's" head falling off during the parade...)

Clipper and Polly greet each new arrival like long-lost friends, winning them over in an instant, then running to fetch either their crushed plastic juice bottle or a mangy tennis ball and dropping it at their feet and staring at it till someone gets the message and flings it for them. It sure is easier to be around this work site hive with these pups as my ambassadors to our motley support crew, the numbers of which increase every day.

A Ranger was posted outside my driveway chain, thankfully, almost all day, to keep the curious from getting under foot. I was grateful for the respite from narrating the goings-on and from having to present my disappointment publicly on the very day it has so intensified. Conrad N. had a good idea: to relate the essentials of the story as simply and convincingly as possible in the form of a Q&A outline.

Q. So, is your house going to be moved too?

A. No, not at this time.

Q. Why?

A. Because the Park didn't make their decision in time...

No, that's not it... Because the Park still hasn't decided to allow me to move it, and now it's too late to go along on this "ride."

Then maybe I should turn the Q&A around and when the questioner asks "Why haven't they decided that?" or "What's the hang up?" I could answer:

"Well, if it were your house and you spent $80,000 to move it, would you expect to be able to continue to own it when it was relocated?"

And if, for many years, you had cooperated to allow the federal government to own a patch of land in the middle of your yard to keep their Lighthouse on, would it seem reasonable to ask them to repay the favor and now allow you to own a patch in their yard for your Lighthouse Keeper's Cottage?"

It's an ad campaign — an oral ad campaign — and here's where all that marketing management, advertising strategy, and design training and experience from my corporate past might finally prove useful.

Sunday, November 3, 1996: *Today's crowd-control Ranger seemed ever so supportive of my campaign to keep my house for some extraordinary number of years if it ever gets moved across the street — maybe even till the ocean uproots us all again. It became clear why she was so supportive: her family owns a home on Cable Road that's subject to one of those "use and occupancy" agreements signed when the Park was established in 1961. Their house was built in '59, but the legislation calling for these people to lose their houses if the Seashore felt they were non-essential, was for some reason made retroactive to 1959, catching their dwelling in its net.*

I just never could understand why the Park had any say over stuff that was here when they came into being, unless it was clearly a non-conforming, incompatible structure such as a clam shack eyesore or a pig farm junk heap sort of thing. But people's summer homes? Even some folks' primary residences? What was so bad about them that provision needed to be made to eventually seize and remove or demolish them?

What will the Park ever do with all these houses and all those evicted neighbors who will damn well leave the Seashore with acid on their tongues and ready to rumble? So <u>what</u> if it's legislated — when legislation requires inhumanity to one's fellow man, the damn legislation should be changed. Lord knows laws are changed every day for lesser public benefit and for poorer logic than <u>this</u>.

Times have significantly changed since 1961. Park budgets (required to manage this windfall of real estate) decrease every year and staffing does too. I can just imagine driving by my old empty home falling to rack and ruin because the Park just took it, simply because a 1961 law said they could. I'd have my slingshot with me!

The Relighting of Highland Light (Sunday evening, November 3, 1996, as recalled Thursday November 7, 1996)

The day was wintry, the blue-gray sky piled at the edges with drama in the form of clouds. The sunlight from noon on would have been warming if it had been calm instead of brutally windy — especially on the highlands of Truro where the relighting of the relocated lighthouse was scheduled for 5 p.m. Rick L, earlier in the day, seemed surprised that I didn't know we had a week earlier passed the deadline by which we needed to have the Seashore's approval for my house to go along on this Lighthouse relocation. It had taken all afternoon for me to get over that small bomb, but by 3:30 I was ready to head north to assure myself a parking space somewhere near the big white tent to the west of the brilliant new-looking Cape Cod Light. When I arrived at 4, the wind was so strong it whipped sand around as if in a desert, so I queued up for a trip to the top of the tower with dozens of other like-minded locals. At the top, the open lantern service gallery door framed a pre-sunset view I shall never ever forget: the sun burned like cold gold, limning the great gray cumulus bank above the icy silvered bayside water. The gray sky, in contrast, now held purple and lavender tones as the golden limning began to turn bright orange. A painting of this sunset would have been judged a fiction; it was so theatrical.

I found a seat in the 12th row (of about 50 rows) of chairs under the tent, and soon the Coast Guard Academy Glee club, the Idlers, began an assortment of patriotic and sea songs as the tent filled with SRO's and we all awaited the dignitaries' arrival. At 5:00, we heard the skirl of the Highland Scottish Pipe Band of Truro, who, in their kilts, with bright red knees, piped in the bigwigs followed by the Coastie Color Guard. All the functionaries were introduced, we sang the national anthem and bowed for a benediction, and then the speechifying commenced. All spoke briefly, sharing history and wit and heaping kudos on the folks who did the relocating and those who paid them to do it. Congressman Studds was awarded a retirement medal for faithful and constant service to the Coast Guard in this area, where they are the most respected (and essential) service. He promised his speech would take less time than the reading of his commendation did, but no one held him to it, as he was such an entertaining and sincere speaker. And then it was time to relight the Light and the countdown to switch-on was joined by the 500 people inside and outside the tent. At "nautical twilight" — on that day ~5:38 p.m. — the premier lighthouse on Cape Cod, 200 years young next year, once again swept the sky with its steady double beacon just about a year after it went dark.

Afterwards, I made my way over to Congressman Studds' assistant and stated briefly that I had just learned that we'd missed the "relo" at Nauset.

"Oh, long time ago," he said. "Didn't you know that?" (triggering for me graphic and unmentionable thoughts — and I've been singing your praises?)

"May I shake your boss's hand?" I said instead, as he was obviously parting the crowd for the Congressman as the TV crews attempted to usher him outside for some interviews.

"Sure," allowed the aide and introduced me to Himself, a very tall fellow (with the deepest most sonorous voice this side of the Lincoln Center).

"Your summary of the Nauset Light situation was so poetic," he said. "Well done!"

"Thank you," I replied. "Now I hope we'll be able to <u>make</u> something of it, and I certainly thank you for helping me do so, because I don't seem to be able to get anywhere on my own," or something to that effect. There followed noises of supportive timbre, and I vowed to follow them, and this, with a fax from New Hampshire, where I would be by 10:30 p.m. if I got out of the crowd early.

As I turned from admiring the Light one last time, hoping to take away from it a vision to light my own darkened light station yard, I began walking down the access road next to a very tall older Coast Guardsman whose Navy trench coat covered his distinguishing symbols of rank as well as his name badge. I struck up a conversation anyway, without real motive, just admiring the ceremony and the feat it commemorated. But as the walk lengthened and my shameless campaigning spirit rose, I ended up stating the case for the wisdom of the 1956 Coast Guard administration to be followed by the 1996 National Park Service — that they agree to tolerate an island of private land within their replacement light station as we private land holders on the other side of the street have happily tolerated the Coast Guard's lighthouse island in our yard for the past 40 years.

"It's just so logical," I concluded. "I just don't see what's wrong with it!"

"Maybe it's too logical," he said. "In any case, I'll keep my fingers crossed for you."

Would that the crossed fingers of the First District Commander were sufficient to solve this knotty problem. But alas, it is not. My only consolation at being left behind, as the Nauset Light migrates across the street next week, is that the abandoned Keeper's House will stand as a stark illustration to the story I can now tell publicly.

Thursday, November 7, 1996: Thursday dawned gray but mild and the crew began assembling at 7 a.m. in what's left of the side yard between here and my next door neighbors. First thing I noticed were the two big "window" squares cut out of each side of the exposed Lighthouse foundation — east and west, for the big cross steel (secondary I-beams) to be slid through like skewers. Had the foundation been orange it would have

142

looked like a flat concrete jack-o'-lantern with a red and white stovepipe hat. Bob and Mike set up to complete the two matching windows in the opposite side, the ocean side, where excavation is being minimized to avoid compromising the tower's stability on the "weak" cliff-side. A horizontal line connecting the two window openings on the west side hinted at the plan: to saw through the foundation once the cross steel and the main 18-inch square H-beams are in place (the latter running north-south above? below? the cross steel I-beams) and the jacking of the tower is ready to begin.

About two feet of the octagonal footing will be left behind, though the Powers That Be require it to be busted up and carted away, rather than what we've suggested: that it be left to migrate gravitationally down/through the eroding cliff face to the beach where it — like the Centre Beacon's brick ring foundation — can be alternately covered and uncovered by the tides. But of course we can't do that! Someone might get hurt! (By a one-ton object "falling" at a rate of some 50 feet in 75 years???) While one of the guys used the diamond-bitted chainsaw from the outside in, the other used a plain old shovel to toss more fill from the inside out the "window" holes, creating a deeper and deeper "basement" below the excavated floor of the tower.

At about 10 a.m., a huge flatbed truck from Maryland pulled up, loaded with the cross steel and H-beams for the Oil House move — which will commence tomorrow — and two-thirds of the dolly-jacks which will be used for the Lighthouse relocation. Expert House Movers' big bulldozer, with an enormous chain hooked in the snaggled teeth of its bucket, offloaded these wonders one by one under the slow, shambling, stoic direction/execution of two great big guys in coveralls. As each dolly assembly — which resembles a landing-gear section for a 747 jumbo jet — was lifted from the truck, it articulated in multiple directions, loose as a goose and live as a big fish until plunked down in my side desert. (You can't call it a "yard" anymore!)

143

Dolly jacks on which Nauset Light was mounted for relocation move across the street to current site.

After lunch break, on returning from running a few errands, we (pups and I) found Mike Bobcat-excavating on the ocean side of the Oil House. Jerry (one of the several brothers who own and run Expert House Movers) and Valerie took a few moments to explain to me the other, more major destruction that was about to begin, i.e., removal of the lawn <u>ALL</u> around the lighthouse and the death-by-dozer of almost all of Miriam's autumn olive bushes. (Oh, maybe they'll leave me the one by the south sidewalk, just so I can recall what's been trashed.) The young Corps of Engineers overseer said, "We're not destroying your bushes, we're improving your view!" Fine, but when that iron dozer maw fastened on to the biggest of those shrubs (which only looked dead in winter but are intensely alive), I almost succumbed to tears. Yet I did not come inside but stayed out in hopes that my presence would exert a "conserve-ive" effect, should the process tend to excess.

By day's end, there was a wide 3–4-foot-deep dirt moat around the tower, and, yes, I could see the ocean from my porch.

I am being adamant about saving the one little tree I can: the little juniper the birds or rabbits planted on the point across the driveway from the Oil House. In 15 years, it has become a 4-foot shrub, and I will not just let them rip it out and toss it aside. But where to tell them to transplant it? Espe-

144

cially since I can ask them to move it just once. Maybe down by the rose bushes at the roadside, where the elder pine died and then fell apart this spring. My one success at saving something besides Oil House bricks, which are secreted away in the cellar — safe, I hope, from the competing local scavengers I've identified so far.

Valerie told me today that the seemingly nice old couple from Dennis that we've seen around here lately and frequently, have been banned from the site even though they bring their own "brain buckets" (hardhats), as they are suspected of taking photos for resale to lighthouse-maven magazines, "scooping" the legitimate press. At the Highland Light relo site they became infamous the day they were spotted up on the gallery peering over the rail, taking video pictures of the actual move from above. I am so lucky to be welcomed to the front lines here. I think I wish I were videotaping it, although I'm glad, really, that I'm not. It's a lot more fun to experience what's going on than to see it all through some tiny viewfinder. I know the Cape Cod Times is here taping from time to time — and I know I'll be able to buy a copy of the resultant videocassette later.*

*The lighthouse relocation was recorded on video produced and released in 1998 (Greg O'Brien and Chuck Kraemer) and is available through the Nauset Light Preservation Society (nausetlight.org).

Friday, November 8, 1996: *The pace sure picked up here today. At mid-morning, the crew had three earthmovers going at once — the Bobcat, the Case 1155 tracked dozer, and a big-wheeled Komatsu dozer (which had finished burying the Oil House's brand new foundation to protect it during the Lighthouse relocation maneuvers across the street.) The earth everywhere on this property shook and the house windows rattled, as the final excavation of all the Coast Guard's dirt around the tower and Oil House was completed (without any more tree loss, thank God).*

The Komatsu's last task was to "round off the corner" out where the lone cedar had stood, guarding the Two Sisters' lintel stones. So, the first step was to relocate the cedar to where the lintels landed last week, down by my wellhead. Bob dutifully dug it up and then Mike loaded it into the Bobcat's scoop and drove it down the driveway, buckling and skewing the old asphalt to a fare-thee-well. At about the same time, Jerry was using the Case 1155 to push the diesel hydraulic generator back into place, with the help of Joe, the huge guy who was moving the thing quite all right by his burly self, but in service of hitching it to the 1155's maw, instead of just pushing it the other way to its desired position, succeeded in carving more huge divots out of driveway and lawn.

"You guys need just a little ATV or something," I said, "to move things like this around here without tearing up everything with these overpowered giants."

"We don't know from 'little'," said Jerry, as he went on tearing up my sidewalk and all the valiant groundcover that has taken over for the wimpy "lawn" over the past 10 years. Sho' nuff don't! If they dropped a quarter, they'd pick it up with a front-end loader just for the challenge!

But what I must push myself to remember, I guess, is that when the relocating is over, I get to supervise the reclamation of all that's been decimated. Valerie says she'll see if Rick will spring for some Russian olives to replace those ripped full-grown out of the earth yesterday. I should also request more hardy stuff than hydroseed in my north side yard, or I'll have to get me a John Deere lawn tractor, says Bob.

As the earth-moving was being done, Bob and Mike were setting up the guides for cutting the most tricky "window slots" in the lighthouse foundation walls, i.e., the two that will cut parallel to the existing holes through the angled facets of the octagon — thus needing to penetrate not 12–14" of wall, but 17–22" of wall — and maybe a foot more when going through the solid stairs that evidently were poured as part of the foundation. Plane geometry put to practical — and critical — use.

Just then, two video crews arrived, one after another — the first, from Israel (!!), the Israeli counterpart to the National Geographic magazine — who learned of our move via the NLP's website and came over expressly to film this. Unfortunately, this is their last day before returning home, but they interviewed Seashore, NLPS, and Chimney and Expert reps (and *ended up hearing my speech, too). The other crew was from Channel 11, Cape News TV, S. Yarmouth.*

As the Israeli team said goodbye, I said, "Tell Benjamin Netanyahu to settle down and cool off."

To which they replied, "We're not saying anything to Benjamin Netanyahu, we dislike him so much." I told him we'd pray for their peace, which they surely do as well.

The Expert company's guys cut/poked/chipped the 3 east-west holes and 2 north-south holes in the subterranean (formerly) extension of the Oil House walls and inserted all the cross steel, resting on two heavy north-south outrigger I-beams. Then they dug out under the beams' ends at each of the Oil House's protected corners and began installing cribbing floors (made of parallel contiguous 6 x 6 oak chunks 4 feet long) for the hydraulic jacks to sit on. When each jack was in place, braced against the beam-end, Jerry, in the control truck, turned the 4 valves to raise the pressure in the 4 hydraulic lines until each was at maximum extension. Then, the corner men installed like Lincoln Logs more cribbing to reach the beam and hammered in wedges to take up the jacks' support task. The jacks were removed, their lines bled so they could contract to minimum height once again, and they were reinstalled on interior cribbing to again contact the beam. In this manner, the little Oil House was raised 4 times to a height of 4 feet above the ground, and the bottom sections of its walls just fell away from about door sill level.

Darkness fell at about this time, so the actual relocation of the structure will be done tomorrow morning. The day's last amazing feat was Richard's backing of the enormous flatbed equipment trailer off Nauset Light Beach Road into my north-side desert, and into position to be backed under the jacked-up Oil House for its removal forever from my yard.

The very thought of losing this little neighbor of mine brought tears to my eyes several times during the jacking and cribbing process, to the point where I couldn't speak. I am as devoted to this structure as I would be to a pet — and much more so than I am to my antique automobile. And

147

tomorrow it will leave and never return. Perhaps we'll someday be neighbors again across the street, and I learned today how much I would like that.

This morning at sunrise I had stood at my bedroom window trying to imagine what it will be like without the Lighthouse in the front yard and I was surprised to anticipate the strong sense of abandonment and vulnerability accompanying that vision. It was startling. Never again will the beam of Nauset light caress the walls of this Keeper's bedroom. It may shine on the guest room walls, but then one will never again be able to lie in the outermost guest bed and be comforted by that bright red and white beacon — my first and strongest remembrance of the first night I spent here in late December 1981.

This is truly the End of an Era here, and when I let myself sit with that thought for more than a sidelong moment, I feel the deepest sadness. It's like a death in the immediate family.

Outside my bedroom window, a south/southeast/southwest blow begins, rumored to reach gale force by tomorrow. The sea, whitecaps as far as the eye could see today (under blue skies), roars up on the unusually flat summer-like beach, and the stars are our last inkling of this clear, windy day. The high temp tomorrow will be an unseasonable mid-60s, followed on Sunday by a precipitous fall into figures cold enough to allow snow. Well, as long as it doesn't lift the Oil House off its cribbing, either here during its last night with me or tomorrow as it stands ignominious and vulnerable off to the side in the Seashore parking lot. My beloved "O." I will miss you surprisingly much. I'm just so sorry that to save you, I have had to let you go.

Saturday, November 9, 1996: *The pups and I were up at sun-trying-to-be-up, and as it broke through the stack of cloud-cribbing on the east horizon, the day turned gorgeous for "Li'l O's" trip to the parking lot. When O.H. was on the bed, Joe fired up the cab's engine — which makes a wicked big tractor sound — and the trip was begun. I perched across the street high up in the trees by the construction fence gate and watched as* the tractor emerged from the dirt alley, pulling, at the way back of the trailer, its precious, still vulnerable-looking treasure. As it pulled fully into Nauset Light Beach Rd. who should appear behind it, now condemned to a snail's pace trip to the donut shop, but up-street neighbor elderly Lillian, the very woman who was so up-in-arms about how long the Lighthouse move would be blocking the road, as her husband is an invalid. I ran over to her window to assure her it would be only a few-minute delay. "You want me to push it?" she asked. "No thanks," I said, happy she was amused.

The first of the three Nauset Light Station structures to be relocated, the Oil House was temporarily taken to the Nauset Light Beach parking lot until after the Lighthouse was moved (November 1996) before being re-sited at its new location.

Then I resumed my place in the parade, thanking my hard hat for allowing me a mobile front row seat right up there with my precious pal the Oil House. At one point, just one quarter of the way down the street, I heard Pam N say, "Tell Mary the guy in the truck wants to see her." When I heard the message, I thought it was "Some guy in a truck" and I scoffed at the intrusion into this thing I would absolutely NOT allow anything to distract me from. Some guy in a truck, indeed.

149

"I think it's the guy in <u>this</u> truck," Hawkins said, so I hopped-to and trotted down to the cab where Joe called, "Come here. Come on up here. I want you to take this wheel." HOLY SMOKE! Yes, <u>Sir</u>! And I held the big flat wheel in both hands, reaching and leaning in from the top step, and the two of us — darned if we didn't steer that truck down to the turn off into the parking lot! "You watch Jerry and when he says go right, you turn right," said Joe... tho' he left me to discover he also meant KEEP turning right. But we did OK! And I was just so tickled! Gee whiz!

When we got to the harder part, entering the lot, I resumed my left rear quarter lookout as we closed in on some fence posts with our crossbeams.

Once we reached the designated spot, the guys placed crib-thickness extended planks of 3-, 4-, and six-inch-square thickness under all the trailers' wheels to boost it over the post tops. Once through and clear, Joe pulled the truck to the far southwest corner and backed the trailer into the last two east-west parking spaces. Then, using small hand-levered jacks, they elevated the Oil House a sufficient smidgen of height so the truck could pull out from under it, then inserted enough mini-cribbing (shingles & wedges) to make up the difference.

Lastly, as the predicted front moved in like a freight train from the east, the guys unrolled a skirt of orange plastic snow fencing to keep the curious from walking underneath or climbing up the cribs. That was my idea — also Jane's — and although it was at first rejected, it's just good that they gave L'il Oily some privacy after being quite happily used to her reclusive life in the pines for the last 15 years. Lord knows all that will change when she makes her final trip (for now) to the new Lighthouse site and is installed on her new foundation (sensible shoes for an elderly lady). The NLPS folks think they can use her as a tiny interpretive site, holding pictures and maybe a video of the move. I'll go console her after hours and we'll reminisce about how idyllic things used to be on this quieter side of the street.

Tuesday, November 12, 1996: *Back at the destruction site following an ever-so-brief "stealth" visit to Lyme, NH, to write and file the Class Notes* *column for the spring issue of the Bryn Mawr Alumni magazine. I left here at 8:30 a.m. on Monday — Veteran's day — and was back here at 9:30 a.m. this morning, having abandoned the choked into-Boston arteries and taking the longer but less congested I-495 South from about Lowell to I-195 at Bourne.*

It's a gorgeous sunny-but-cumulated day here, with the temp in the 40°F range, a more hospitable clime than Lyme's cloudy with flurries. I arrived to find the base cribbing installed beneath the huge main beams and jacks already in place to boost the four cross-steel members inserted perpendicular to them and neatly skewering the top 2/3 of the tower's foundation, through those hard-won holes which Mike and Bob had spent 10 days creating.

Outside in my front yard (at 10 p.m.) is the most astounding site. The workers left a clamp light on, attached to one of the cross-steel beams in the tower, and its beam is casting the eeriest glow in all directions from beneath and within the structure. At one spot it looks (through the open door) as if there is a glowing hearth against the far curve of the wall. The red iron stair section above it casts a cold black shadow below its curled spiral. And as the tower is now perched on its wide light colored crossbeams with a good 18" of air between the top 2/3 and the bottom 1/3 of its foundation, it seems (against the coal black star spangled sky) to be hovering about two feet above the hole in the ground it used to sit in. If you start your gaze at the darkened lantern top and let your eyes slowly travel down the dimmed shape of the Lighthouse, when you get to the eerie glow beneath it, it looks like a giant rocket frozen in mid-launch.

Seeing that 150-ton tower rise slowly on its I-beams this afternoon, its foundation silently parting at the arduous saw cut, was otherworldly. In the back of my mind, I had been thinking about escape routes if it started to tip, but when it moved so evenly and slowly and silently, I realized it would take a massive failure of a proven system to cause me to need such a plan.

Tomorrow they'll raise the entire assembly to a height of 7 ft. above grade and put the dollies on either side, beneath the main beams. Then the legendary red "fifth wheel" dolly-truck will arrive and get set to haul the Light north across the yard to where the Oil House stood. By Thursday, the colossus will be at the street, ready for ComElectric's crew (probably the same ones who tried to shut off my house service last Thursday) to lower the lines and let the assembly cross the street to the new site.

My latest startling remark to folks is that the Nauset Lighthouse and the Keeper's House — the customary and distinguishing pair of recognizable and beloved structures — will, as of Friday, no longer fit in the same single viewfinders of tourists' cameras. We considered doing up a panoramic shot that would fit both structures into it — a print necessarily over a foot long — and printing thousands of them up with the message "What is wrong with this picture?"

Today out by the street I met Pete Friesen, the self-made man who invented, patented, and currently manufactures the integrated hydraulic jacking system that Expert and ICC now use in almost all their jobs. What a sweet guy. If you met him on a bus, you'd think he was a retired minister: self-effacing, soft-spoken, modest, and polite with crinkly eyes and white hair and a strongly Canadian accent. He and Jerry came into the house for a beer after work tonight and it was nice to see the rougher, risqué Jerry demur to the older, wiser grandfather-figure, as the latter explained his system to us, startling us with how non-proprietarily he treats his work, sharing techniques and equipment with his keenest competitors. He is truly a "class act." I would feel honored to work with him.

Wednesday, November 13, 1996: I heard yesterday from Hawkins that the Superintendent was making noises as if she is ready to give me the Park's official response or counterproposal to my unofficial draft proposed July 9, 1996, at the time when she had instructed me to "Pick a number of years, ninety-nine is too many," then went back to the 25 they had proposed 2 years ago. I have been here 15 of the past 18 days — and I have answering machines at both bases (here and NH), so I am not too hard to find.

But now, in the cold hard light of dawn, I think it's time to anticipate the worst and prepare for it, so that my reaction will not be wholly inappropriate. I am guessing that they will offer some minor amount towards the value of the house itself, and then make me choose between lifetime tenancy and 25 years.

Assuming their offer is for a low cash amount, to move across the street onto public land, giving up ownership of my house, and having a lease with a tenancy of 25 years, my concerns:

- I've never been in this for the money — but, historically, even non-conforming users back in 1961 (when CCNS bought folks out) were paid for the value of not just the house but the whole property. So, I'll presumably be stuck forever paying taxes on my current land until the road beam is under mean low tide.
- I'm locked in and wouldn't be able to sell the house or pass it on to wealthier heirs, nor can I borrow against it or work out any other deal, even with a potentially better funded Park Service in the future.
- MANY sticking points remain unresolved — how can I live in a house whose land I don't own? Who owns my well? My septic system? My driveway? And who insures it and handles disasters and/or liability claims? Who owns the 1926 Keeper's garage? Can I rebuild on my left-behind foundation? Use my well? My septic system? If not, why not?
- If I owned the House, I'd willingly assume the burden of major repairs and maintenance. I'd also be assuming the hassle of being in a far more vulnerable-to-vandalism situation.
- I'll presumably have no say in any disagreements or disputes.

In fact, the more I consider staying on this site to see what may happen with NPS policy and funding in the next 2 years, and to lengthen my tenure as owner of the place by stalling until the clock has to start, the more I realize I have just donated to the government some considerable number of years/months in this patch's longevity by allowing ICC to strip *half of it of its stabilizing ground cover, shrubbery, and trees. And they PLAN to merely hydroseed it when they leave!!?!*

I don't think so. Their legally permitted access was/is limited to "via the driveway" (which is now mostly gone). I think they owe me some bear-berry, pin-cherry, juniper, scrub oak, beach plum, rosa rugosa, and bayberry to replace what they've decimated — and I'm determined to say so.

————

Yesterday's sunset, in a sky just brimming with cumuli, was spectacular. It was another day when a lid of clouds had sat overhead until sundown, when the reddening sun slipped free at the edge to suffuse everything with silver and gold, while the pink in the east cloud banks intensified against the now blue sky. There have been three such spectacular sunsets here recently: October 28, when the deconstruction of Nauset Light began with that whole double rainbow just offshore; Sunday, Nov 3d, which I saw from the top of Highland Light just before the relighting ceremony; and last night's, as this tower rose off its foundation.

This morning, I heard the Cape Cod Construction guy talking just outside my window to the USA Corps of Engineers project overseer, about "widening the corner at the street," so the tower move won't face such an acute turn as it leaves my property and cuts across to the new "haul road." I leaped into my clothes and jogged down the driveway to see just what "widening the corner" meant, fearing the loss of still more of my trees. Sure enough, two 12-foot cedars and a really nice young bushy oak (that resembles an old apple tree, without its foliage) had been pointed out as goners. I got fairly riled and said I was just not going to sit still for this, having never been consulted about further deci-mation. What had already been done was far more than would have been possible had I stuck to the letter of the law and made ICC take the tower out along the existing agreed-upon (in 1981) right-of-way — down the driveway. Although he gave me a bit of resistance at first, ulti-mately he confided, "If they'd told me they were going to take all the trees out of my yard and replace 'em with grass, I would have complained too."

Damn right. Evidently this trees-for-grass exchange was okayed within the acceptance of ICC's bid — even though nothing was ever said to me about the reclamation details, just that the "damage would be repaired," or something equally vague. The Corps of Engineers overseer says that since I'll be saving them some cost by giving up my driveway around the house, we can have a talk with Hawkins about NLPS contributing some native groundcover shrubs and trees to the reclamation, but he made it clear that the labor beyond grading would have to be done — and paid for — without using ICC/EXPERT painters, probably by Cape Cod Construction or nursery/landscaping laborers. I myself am envisioning a community volunteer "labor day" to restore the old site to some degree of naturalness. (I am sure that if CCNS had lost a patch of native ground cover and shrubs/trees to a private construction project, they would unquestionably require replacement and restoration — why shouldn't this be the same?)

There's been a red, curly tailed, tall eared, pointy snooted stray dog around the yard ever since the crew arrived — we assume it's been abandoned by summer people who fed him up until a couple of weeks ago. He is so skinny you can count, even from a distance, not only his ribs but his vertebrae. He's standoffish around people — won't come closer than 10 yards or so — but he seems accustomed to coming nearer the EHM crewmen while they're busy building cribs for the jacks. So, I encouraged one of them to fill his pockets with biscuits this morning, and sure enough, when the little stray came around and he tossed him a few, the little dog eagerly scarfed them up. So, I went in and fetched a bowl of dry chow, followed by a bowl of water, and he chowed down out there in a front loader furrow. Later, in the afternoon, he returned for just a bite more but wouldn't come any closer. I'll keep feeding him — and I'm leaving the garage door 1-½ feet open during tonight's 30° weather — and we'll talk him up to all the bystanders this weekend. Maybe someone will leave here with a live souvenir of the relocation! That would make me really happy — one really good, lasting thing coming out of all this destruction and abuse.

Wonder of wonders: this afternoon I found a friendly and surprisingly hopeful message from the CCNS Superintendent on my answering machine. Now this may be all fog and no rainbow, so I won't let myself get all excited about it. But in it, she said that she wanted me to know that she's still very actively working on this whole question about what to do with my house and that she wanted to reassure me that it is "right at the top of her to-do list — and has been every day for months." And, that she feels embarrassed when I am quoted in the newspaper as saying that I am "still in negotiations with the Park Service" and she wants me to know that "you ARE still in negotiations with the Park Service," ... and that they are working hard to find the best possible answer for the Keeper's House.

————

The Lighthouse now hovers about 5-½ feet above the leave-behind lower 1/3 of its foundation, and all the cribs (4 outside, 2 inside) are in position to accommodate the insertion of those aircraft-landing-gear, rubber-tire dollies tomorrow. Tonight's guests after work in the Keeper's House kitchen included Jerry and his four guys: Mike, Rick, Bobby, and Joe. None would sit down for fear of getting the furniture dirty, so we stood in the kitchen and drank beer and Doctor Pepper and told a few stories till they had to head out to eat. Some took me up on the offer of self-guided tours of the Keeper's House. I think it's neat that they're curious about the <u>insides</u> of structures as well as the outsides. And I wish someone were <u>audio</u> taping this move, never mind video recording it.

Thursday, November 14, 1996: *Sitting in Chatham Ford's service waiting room while my Explorer gets her "pan dropped," I have a moment to record the morning's events. Fortunately, I'm not missing anything at the Lighthouse right now, since the red truck with a third dolly-jack role in this play hasn't yet arrived from Rhode Island. I asked Mike why it wasn't here yet and he said it was being painted. When I asked why it needed painting, he said, "Because we dropped a house on it." Of course, he was kidding — <u>all</u> these guys have my number now, it seems!*

So, this morning the crew could go only as far as placing the dollies on either side of the main beams between cribs and clamping them onto it with (mere) C-clamps. Chuck K from Channel 5 in Boston (an ABC affiliate) was on site and so we redid a bit of Tuesdays interview, which I'm quite glad had too much bulldozer noise in the background for his taste. (That was literally a "bad hair day" for me. Of course, a man wouldn't care about that but it was SO bad, I was reminded of the "little girl/who had a little curl/right in the middle of her forehead." My words were fine — in fact more eloquent than previously, but I think I looked a fright. Gee, if I ever got the silver tongue and the silken locks to coincide on the same day, I think I'd be dangerous!

"Keeper," our site stray — whom I'm calling half Australian dingo and half Egyptian pharaoh hound — came much closer today and ate two servings of chow from his bowl on the second step of the porch. Sherry, a photographer from the Cape Codder, took his picture and said they'd do a little sidebar with a headline "Do you know this dog?" Perhaps as a media star he'll find a good home, or his rightful owners, although I'd call his owners downright WRONGful if they knowingly left him behind when they closed up their cottage for the winter.

Today's most spectacular photo opportunity came when Jerry said to me, "You want a unique shot? Get in the bucket." He was sitting in the CASE 1155 driver's seat and I scrambled haltingly, nervously, into the ice cold bucket and sat down, chilling my backside for the day! "No, no," he said, "Stand up. Hey, Rick, get in the bucket and stabilize it." We both stood in the general purpose bucket and Jerry elevated us like on a Ferris wheel about 25 feet off the ground while I nervously snapped a couple of shots with Joe's camera — mine was out of film, of <u>course</u>. Just then Valerie, the site superintendent, came walking up the side hill with Hawkins and hollered, "You better not let anybody see this, Jerry, or we'll all have ourselves in a sling. We'll be shut down!" Thankfully, I never got above the roof peak, so none of the assembled "street people" saw me. The shot wasn't really all that special — about what I can see from the Keeper's bedroom *window, actually. And I was a little nervous, having sneaked a peek behind us down to earth... but it <u>was</u> an adventure!*

The best photo viewpoint (I hope I got it...) was from directly beneath the center of the Lighthouse tower, looking up through the double window-sized hole in the floor that Mike and Bob had spent days punching through. My neighbors from across the street and from next door came over, and we took turns, one at a time, posing beneath the Lighthouse step-overhang and the northernmost crossbeam as if we were holding the Light above our heads in Atlas-like poses. Silly, silly, silly... and all illustrative of how a construction site and proximity to heavy equipment turns an adult into a kid again. VROOM, VROOM!!!

First thing this morning, the guys said, "Hey, you see your picture in the paper today?" I still haven't, but I understand it's an aerial shot by CCT's Steve H of this site, and there I am right by the Light in my yellow jacket and green hard hat. Wait till the kids back home see this.

For some reason, I wasn't full of pithy quips and arresting analogies this morning when Chuck K was interviewing me. But now, 12 hours later, I am thinking that I have a tendency to pack my summing-up remarks with too much detail, rendering them unnecessarily unwieldy and complex instead of keeping them as stunningly simple and logical as they inher-ently could be. I should simply say, "For 40 years, two civilians have graciously accommodated the presence of the United States Government on a small patch of federal land in the midst of our private property. All I'm asking is that this favor now be repaid: that the federal government allow their former host reciprocal accommodation on a small patch of private land in the middle of their federal reservation across the street — on what is to be the new Nauset Light Station for the next hundred years."

However, it seems that the Park Service has been offering me almost that, i.e., a place in their federal reserve for about 40 years... IF I can manage to live that long. (Yo! FATE! Listen up!) Except they're not allowing me to OWN the property my house will sit on. Hmmm... If that's the only factor missing, what would I say if they conceded that point and left the rest of their takeover proposal (threat) the same? I don't know. Even 40 years doesn't seem like a very long time when these tables are turned.

Friday, November 15, 1996: *The last thought on what's left of my mind last night was how quickly we have all become used to the site of the huge Nauset Light tower suspended by Lincoln Logs 6-½ feet off the face of the earth — even in last night's gale-force gusts and steady icy north/northeast blow. Heck, if we can become accustomed to that, it shouldn't be hard to get used to its complete absence.*

I still wish they'd leave the octagon intact, maybe just cover it over, and leave it to slowly sink down the face of the eroding cliff, to take over in 60 years for the Beacon's brick ring which by then will be underwater all the time. It could be the next generation's archaeological reference marker and I can't imagine it being any more of a hazard to beachgoers than the ring is today. I am, by the way, astounded at how small the octagon looks all by itself sitting in the dirt (now buried in the dirt), so the Big Mack truck, which arrived at 6:10 this morning, can disregard it during the actual move, which begins today.

Though the cab is freshly repainted, it shows its age beneath, behind, and inside the cab. Joe says it's one of the first trucks EXPERT used in starting its business. It is trailered to its jobs to save its immense power for stuff lesser trucks couldn't handle. Besides, Joe says, on the highway it would *bump your kidneys loose. They brought no ramps to unload it with, so they piled a load of my dirt by the side of the street with the old beast, the 1155, and offloaded it onto that. How resourceful, except that they nipped the already-once-repaired NYNEX line in two places doing so, so I'm out of phone service for a while.*

The 651 rubber-tired forklift loader, "OSWALT" with its swiveling midsection joint, is now removing all the unused cribbing from my site over to the new site of the Light and Oil House. Joe flattened the roadway from the old Oil House site to the road with the 1155, and late yesterday, two more cedars (but not my oak!) were marked to be brutally plucked from the south corner of that Desert Alley, setting the way for the first half of the trip across the street.

Big Red sits patiently atop his cribbing and dollies, with an improving skyscape behind him, now that the snow has stopped whistling by at 40 mph sideways and the sun has come out. The winds were so strong last night, I thought the hovering tower might turn into a musical instrument as they blew across the hole in its floor. (Mike said if that's what we wanted, he'd have left one of the porthole windows open at the top.)

When the missing link beam connector was clamped to the main beams and ends and mounted on Big Mack, and after a small I-beam was bolted to the tongue ends of the two dollies and chained firmly to one of the bigger

cross steel beams, and when the last of the old cribbing was removed and the web of support was set down only on the dollies, Nauset Light was ready to move.

And at 2:12 p.m. it did so: just a few test inches due north. As it did, I must admit I let out a YEOWWW!!! of delighted enthusiasm and was told in friendly but firm terms not to do that again, as it sounded too close to a direction-holler from one of the crew. Oops!

The snow blew on-again-and-off-again out of the very dramatic sky, and when the wind wasn't icing us with snowflakes, it was assaulting us with sand... but the crew continued to function like a well-rehearsed cast, hauling 2 x 6 and 2 x 8 planks out from beneath the wheels of the dollies and Big Mack and placing them in front again, as the iterative slow-motion move began. The big squarish compressor truck was detached from the dolly/lighthouse system (which also had its own braking system bolted up onto the floor of the tower) during the actual forward progress until such time as there needed to be a center-of-gravity compensation adjust-ment, to keep more weight on the inside dolly rather than the ocean side dolly. (Even though that meant if it toppled it would topple onto my house!)

The northward trek was also complicated by the fact that it was up out of a hole on the ocean side — a low point — which meant the tracked front end loader had to pull outboard in concert with Big Mack, via a cable hook through a convenient slot in the leading edge of the ocean side main beam.

When the first forward motion was achieved, then halted, I swear the big tower swayed just as any flatbed cargo might as it settled back down to a stop. THAT was impressive!

My porch was heaped with bodies — video cameramen, still photogra-phers, writers, and reporters plus Ken B, Eastham's building inspector, and my guests Jay and Judith, the newlyweds from Northampton. We were all grateful for the chance not just to see it all from a front-row seat, but also to be shielded somewhat from the relentless north wind. The street was filled with hardy gawkers. The less stalwart among them kept asking the

161

Ranger, all through the afternoon, "So when is it going to start moving?" until it began to turn the corner by the old Oil House site. Its motion, doubtless, was not very discernible to anyone not on site.

It was at about that point, or as we neared it, that Jerry motioned for me to come into the midst of the temporarily stalled action, put my arm through his, and escorted me to the passenger side door of Big Mack and helped boost me up and in. I would RIDE the rest of the to-the-street leg up there in the cab, learning fascinating tidbits like the truck has 44,000 miles on it, all in first gear!! The ultra-low gear we hauled the Light in meant the accelerator pedal was barely used, the engine idle sufficient to bear us along at a proper snail's pace to give the crew time to unbuild aft and rebuild forward the wooden plank road.

"Is somebody following you?" called Jerry from the decimator. And I was suddenly aware at that point that the tall tower was always right behind us, as our wheels slowly made their way forward through the dirt... if it was always right behind us, and if we were moving, then the Lighthouse was surely no longer where it used to be...

Little "Keeper," the site stray, in a show of trust like we'd not seen before, came right up to us and almost wanted to play — a very good sign of returning sociability. Alternatively, he kept loping through the action zone and in and out of my garage, where I had been setting out his dinner. Clearly, he had read the ad and seen his picture on p. 15 of today's issue of the Cape Cod Times, depicting him with the tower behind him, caption beginning with "Owner wanted for a dog with a sense of history and great timing."

After coming back from dinner with friends, I found "Keeper" tucked in at the back wall of my garage, having eaten maybe 1/4 of the 3rd or 4th bowl of dog chow I had put out in the garage for him, leaving the overhead door up/open about two feet. I was able to coax him two lengths into the workshop, but lost him again in an attempt to make sure he didn't have to sleep out in this 29° night. Later, I returned to the garage and managed to close the overhead door, then somehow cajoled him into coming far enough (4 lengths) into the basement so I could close that door too, and assure him a much cozier corner than in my garage. He even did two "play bows" before he sat down next to me and let me pat him, tentatively, while he held his breath. I know he's asleep at the top of the cellar stairs now. And wonder of wonders, at about 8:00 p.m., I received a phone call from a prospective owner in response to our "ad" in today's paper: from an MSPCA volunteer — a nice lady from Wellfleet with a German accent who sounds just perfect for "Keeper" and will come to see him on Monday.

Saturday, November 16, 1996: I snapped some pictures of the dawn-lit rosy tower as it sat for one morning only in Desert Alley, till the ComElectric crew arrived at 8 to drop the electric lines and let the move resume. Susan and I had proposed that it was such a privilege to have the newly mobile Lighthouse in one's side yard, even if only for a few hours, that the NLPS should consider leaving it on the truck while driving it around from house to house for a donation of $10K per evening.

At exactly 8:48 a.m., the resumed move took the Nauset Light across my western property line and I could no longer consider it "mine." Out of the cab, I found I could see fifty times more details of the move, and wearing my ICC green helmet, I could get as close as I reasonably dared to all the critical clearances on either side. When invited into the truck the day before, Mike had said he did so because he wanted to keep me pacified

163

while he took out some more trees of mine. But now I was free to defend them — and my lovely silver-gray-and-sage splotched oak tree sacrificed just a limb and not its life, to the cause.

As the truck navigated the S-turn left out of Desert Alley, across Nauset Light Beach Road, and right onto the haul road to its new foundation, I was amazed at its periodic tilting — all calculated, predicted, and allowed-for, but nonetheless disconcerting. The hall road began with a short uphill slant, so the crew resumed their plank-roadbuilding until the truck reached the long level stretch. Rick L, who presented me with my crisp white International Chimney Co. baseball cap, with the transom tagline "A MOVING EXPERIENCE," had feared the new road would be soft all the way to the foundation, requiring another half-day of planking, but once it got going, it fairly glided to the beginning of the downhill approach to the foundation, reaching it by lunchtime. Then the maneuvering began.

Nauset Light being trucked at glacial pace up to new public site across Nauset Light Beach Road.

During the move so far, the truck — and the Light — had gone from a due north course to a due south one, so the tower was now completely 180° turned around, with its door facing south toward the parking lot, not north as it always had at my site. Personally, I would have preferred the door be on the more public side, facing the origin of the pedestrian traffic, but no one asked me, for sure! Instead, in their customary zeal for historic authenticity, the Park Service insisted the tower be oriented exactly as it had been, and now the crew moving it would have to spend half a day maneuvering it around 180° while it sat atop its beams and dollies, in a cul de sac insufficiently spacious to allow the truck pulling it to turn around. (Backing the trailer-like assembly into the "haul road" would have been equally difficult.)

The feat was accomplished by pulling the truck across the new foundation like an arrow through the octagon, then cribbing and jacking the ends of the "missing link" yoke beam up till the truck's eight rear wheels were off the ground, and the whole back of the truck hung from its trailer hitch. Then they looped a chain around the cab's front bumper and one of the 1155 Decimator's bucket teeth and lifted the front wheels off the ground too.

Now, with the truck entirely off the ground, they could rotate the truck counterclockwise from 10:00 to 6:00 — when it would be pointed due north again, and ready to drive out of the octagon. Coincidentally to this hauling of the cab, the dollies' tongues were unyoked and they were reoriented on planks till they were following each other around in the same tight counterclockwise circle so that when the truck was bullied around in two stages, the dolly wheel assemblies would just follow. No orientation vis a vis the footing would change; just the orientation of the tower would. It was so simple, so clever, and so immensely capable an effort, it was mesmerizing.

By dark, everything was pretty much on target — maybe there was a foot or so to nudge it all to get it exactly atop the footer — and the next day's work would mainly involve vertical orientation.

As I walked back down the "haul road" to Nauset Light Beach Road, I looked up just once to see the weird absence of the Light to the right of my house above the windbreak. I could almost not bear to go around the house into the front yard, and was glad to have an excuse not to until after dark: my next-door neighbor had cleaned out her pantry and refrigerator and had set out a nice spread of snacks. Asti Spumante and Budweiser/Miller beer for the crew, and all but Bobby and Joe attended. Stories were told by everyone (including Valerie and her husband who had come up on his weekend off from wrapping up the Bird Island Light repair/repainting job a mile off the coast of Massachusetts.) The most impressive of which was one told by one of the crew who has just celebrated 11 months of sobriety. He was knocked off a water tank job by an electrical jolt that burned him over 25% of his body, he's attempted suicide, was beaten to a pulp by a jealous husband, and later, en route to the hospital to visit his wife, he was involved in a car wreck that put him in the bed next to her in the ICU. All this in one year! This fellow is half cat and about out of lives, I'd submit.

Back here in my kitchen, while "Keeper" scarfed down another couple of dinners, my friends Judith and Jay cooked a wonderful pasta al pesto dinner, accompanied by two kinds of wine a la méthode champenoise. We stayed up far too late for me before I saw them off to their beautiful accommodations at the Whalewalk B&B and the girls and I retired to the sound of a pounding surf — the third straight day of it, as if to underscore the nick-of-time-ness of our Lighthouse relocation.

Nauset Lighthouse safe at new site — with display of gratitude to all (NLPS, CCNS, and community) supporters who made the move possible.

Sunday, November 17, 1996: *Sunday morning dawned clear, windy, and promising to be warmer, and the crew began around 8 a.m. to finalize the positioning of the Light over its footer and the removal of the transport system, i.e., dollies and truck. It was a reverse playback of Friday's awesome adventure, this time with half the attendant awe. By 3 p.m. the truck was gone, and the dollies and yoke were loaded onto the rental tractor-flatbed. And the Nauset Light was suspended about 4-½ feet higher than its final destination of about 2-½ feet above the footer — the gap to be filled in by masons on Tuesday, making the next relocation, in circa 2071, a much easier proposition, as it'll be a whole lot simpler to bust out bricks from the I-beam slots and to separate foundation from footing than it was to cut through concrete, even with the diamond tipped saw blades and chains.*

Tomorrow the little Oil House will be returned to its rightful place — and sensible new support "shoes" — by the tower. Maybe then the final grading can be done to begin the restoration of the war scene that is my front and side yards.

View of landscaping swath cut around Keeper's House by the Lighthouse relocation process.

I wonder if it is too late in the year to expect shrubs and plants — even the hardy native varieties — to survive transplantation. I guess we'll have to wait and see what the nursery people say. If indeed they are not a mere fig leaf of my hopeful imagination.

Monday, November 18, 1996: *Last night, Andy reminded me that Thanksgiving is just 10 days away. Golly, I have certainly been in a timeless fog during the past three weeks.*

Today the Lighthouse was moved another 6 rotated inches to better match up with its octagonal foundation, a maneuver in which the crib-masters (or stack-rats, as they are known) broke out big bars of Ivory soap and colored the tops of the top row of blocks in each crib white, and topped them with similarly coated shims cut from 1/4 inch plywood. Sandwiching the slippery sides together, then setting the main beams down on them, they hauled on the slotted end of one of the main beams with the Decimator and a chain, till the whole Lighthouse and beam assembly made the minimal adjustment. It was miraculously accurate, and the most delicate maneuver I've seen these bulldozer cowboys of the first order accomplish.

When it was "aimed" right, they lowered it about 4-½ more feet in a series of processes that run: jacks tight, down, up, fill-in, jacks down, remove and replace jacks 2 block-widths down, jacks tight, and repeat.

This afternoon, "Little Orly" the Oil House was fetched home from the parking lot and set down to within several inches of its foundation, ready with the Lighthouse for the bricklayer, who's due in next Tuesday.

Sunday Night, November 24, 1996: *This past Wednesday it was ZOOOOM! to New Hampshire, then this afternoon it was back again. It's no wonder that while I was home for those 3 whole days and nights, that in the dark I'd waken and not be quite sure in which direction to set out to find the bathroom or kitchen. I was able to catch up on some critical projects and tie up some loose ends though, and reply to mail and voice messages from close friends who were aware the Lighthouse was being moved and how important a time this was in my life. Some whom I might naturally invite down to visit at the Keeper's House, only now I find that I suddenly am feeling embarrassed about inviting <u>anyone</u> to this Keeper's House, now that it's lost its two raisons d'être, and while its setting is a colossal dust bowl.*

Yet, I am glad to be back, even if I am hearing that the land reclamation won't start tomorrow as planned, but on Tuesday — maybe necessitating yet another trip down here after flying up the interstate for turkey on Thursday at Andy's.

One high point of this trip is fetching little Keeper boy home from the Vet's where everyone raved about him. He looks just fabulous in his beauteous newly shampooed red coat and his handsome new red collar with the shiny heart-shaped rabies vax tag. He was VERY happy to see me, Clipper, and Polly — why, he fairly bounced around here like a jumping jack — upstairs, downstairs, boing boing boing... all the while his long feathery tail whipping back and forth like a busted rudder.

I now have a fairly substantial sum invested in this sweet fellow, but I feel led to do this for him, noting, as I do, that I am including this little stray in my River of Life scenario as a full-fledged member of the human race —my little homeless person —not just as some stray dog. My mistake, I'm sure, but one I am not in the least apologetic about.

Monday, November 25, 1996: *While the masonry crew is bricking-in the 2-½ foot space between the Lighthouse's footing and its antique octagonal foundation, the pups and I are relaxing in our antique sitting room, hoping the furnace warms this big open space up in the absence of sun. What a dreary day, verging on some form of precipitation or other but it's not clear what. In reading the New York Times Sunday Magazine, I find myself looking at some of the real estate ads and wondering... hmm... Maybe if I were to get a fair and reasonable equity payment from the Seashore and not be tied to paying taxes on this east-side-of-the-road lot for forever and a day... Maybe I could see where I might like to close out this Eastham chapter of my life at some point. Maybe the nearer New Hampshire coast would be nice. In other words, for a few short minutes I see that losing this house to an official public future forever and ever (Amen) might not be the end of the world, for me or for my nieces and nephews. I hear the echo of what I have said recently to others: "I feel that my job is just to get the most fair deal that I can from the National Park so that there is no question ever from my family, from my heirs, about my*

*resolve." And I believe it. I can live with it. I can even perhaps someday —
if it's better to — live without it. Live somewhere else.*

*This is different! Why, I think even Miriam would agree that if I give it my
all and my best, whatever compromise results will be an honorable one,
especially given that continued private ownership in perpetuity and
without restrictions is probably unlikely. How nice, as one is being swirled
down a drainpipe, to catch a glint of light off the fixtures from time... to...
time.*

Tuesday, November 26, 1996: *It's only a grade-level monument, the
remaining 1/3 of the Nauset Light's foundation, but it's diamond-polished
and now that I've shoveled it off, it would make a remarkable garden wall.
The huge 3-foot diameter circular saw blade cut through aggregate and
cement with the water-coolant slurry shining the resultant cut smooth as
marble. I wish I could keep it but the Park people feel that, as it migrates
slowly to beach level, it would become an "attractive nuisance" and ultimately, a potential hazard to safety.*

*And this morning the Komatsu Klaw came to do battle with the Octagon
(foundation) which put up tremendous resistance for the first quarter
hour. The claw dug and whanged and pulled and bashed, and at last broke
through the middle of the south facet, and a piece the size of my dresser was
neatly deposited in the waiting dump truck.*

*But the remainder resisted, causing the tracked digger to nearly topple
over forward a couple of times as it tugged with all its might on the
sections adjacent to the break. Evidently, the Lighthouse's foundation was
poured over a nearly solid circular footing of brick and mortar or cement
some 2 to 2-½ feet deep. So, each regularly shaped chunk of foundation
was anchored in the earth by an irregular chunk of brick and cement
amalgam about half again its size and weighted down with earth. It did
not go quietly. When a section too large for the dump truck was unearthed,
the claw raised it as high as possible (two stories) and dropped it on the rest
of the ring, hoping it would break itself into more stowable pieces. All did
but the stair section, which showed evidence of being formed in two pours*

but which wasn't about to relinquish its nearly cubic shape, despite being dropped four or five times.

All the while, the sou'wester blew torrents of rain sideways as the "dumpah drivah," and I stood in shelter on my porch discussing his job and his fourth generation Orleans ancestors. (Everybody's got a story!) Behind us, Clipper, Polly, and "Keeper" crowded onto the stairway to see out the window.

Being here for this most "moving" experience has not only been educational, but also essential, as there was no one on site representing my interests but me... and if I had fun too, so much the better. Two incidents will suffice to illustrate the power-grabbing attitudes of representative factions in a media circus like a Lighthouse move.

One early day, as Bob and Mike were busy sawing the foundation of the Light with that big 3-foot bladed circular saw, I was standing out front chatting with Hawkins (NLPS). Two big red-shirted guys in dungarees came up from the street and announced to Hawk, "We're gonna cut the power to this house now."

"I don't think so," I said. "'Cause these guys are using my electricity and my water to do the job they're doing."

"Those are our instructions," they said, waving a crumpled work order.

"You may be cutting power to the Lighthouse," I said, "but you're NOT cutting power to my house. I live here!"

"Well, that's not what we were told," the big one said sullenly.

"So what," I said. "They told you wrong." I was a bit surprised at my own intolerant tone, but proud of my defense... The two retreated to their ComElectric truck, and Life went on.

Then the day the tower was to cross the road, I was standing at the roadside in my side yard, speaking to Larry, the Corps of Engineers overseer/site engineer, when an officious young Park employee swooped in,

172

reached out to grab Clipper's collar and asserted, "We're taking these two dogs."

"I beg your pardon," said I, incredulously.

"We're collecting two dogs that have been reported wandering loose out here," he said, making a stretch for Polly's collar, too. (She neatly side-stepped his advance and hid behind my legs.)

"Not THESE two," I said.

"Why not?"

"Because they're mine."

"Do they have leashes?" he asked accusingly.

"They have leashes, dog beds, bowls... everything a dog should have," said I.

"Well, why aren't they leashed?"

"Because THEY LIVE HERE!" I said, not a little testily. "This is their yard. They are 'doing their stuff.'"

"Oh well," he huffed, and melted into the assembling crowd.

———

My new answering machine message:

"Thanks for callin' Nauset Light... or what's left of it. Now that the Lighthouse has been stolen, the Keeper's out lockin' the barn door. Leave a message and your number and she'll call you back."

———

Tuesday, December 3, 1996: Today it was interesting to see the Expert House Movers crew again, doing their choreographed final dance across the street — removing the iron toothpicks from the Lighthouse foundation holes and from the little Oil House's holes in its walls. The masons set right to *bricking in the holes and tomorrow (weather willing) the site reparation will resume over there and, later, here. I'll probably return to NH, where we left "Mew" behind this time, hoping all goes well with "Keeper" at his nice new abode over on Thorne Road. I just hope he doesn't think I've simply abandoned him — surely an inequitable outcome of his best-boy behavior. And I hope his new owner will get down-on-the-floor involved in giving him lots and lots of love so he doesn't miss me and try to come back here after we're gone. He is such a perfect little sweetheart. I will love him forever.*

Looking back over the adventure that was my losing Nauset Light, I can say with surety that the high point for me was saving not the structures so much as this remarkable puppy. The raging surf that accompanied the removal to safety seemed to say to us all, "You can run but you can't hide." But the message in those brown almond eyes was, "I'm weary of running and hiding. I want your love." That small wordless message just poured sweetness all over the losses it accompanied. HE was the project I could manage, the need I could fill, while all about me was this awesome, expensive, engineered postponement of inevitable surrender to the will of the waves. "Keeper" was Heaven-sent. I wonder if Miriam applied the postage.

———

"To Jerry, with thanks for the front seat view of the rescue of these treasures... and a dozen minus-points for habitat destruction."

This inscription says it all to the wild man who drove this moving crew and entertained us all at the same time, Jerry M, who had the good taste and brass whatevers to ask for two copies of my book. (I think he volunteered to pay for them, but what kind of an ingrate would accept that offer?) I only wish that while all those others were videotaping the relo that I had been able to AUDIO tape it. Over the next few weeks, I'll hope the video footage and still photos I will collect will help me recall just half the stories contained in and recited during the past few weeks by this ultra-colorful crew.

As we shared a beer and some more life stories, Jerry said, "You HAD those guys, you know. When we all talked about how the move would be done, they told us, 'It sits right in the middle of her yard, y'know. And tho' she seems like a nice lady, if she says it don't go, it don't go!'"

That's nice to know. I suppose. Although I heard myself explain that I expected that my good will shown in accommodating their wishes to move it the roundabout way might get me points in my battle with the Seashore for a land swap. Even as I spoke, however, it sounded illogical and unlikely that the two situations were related or linked by anything but the River of Life.

Que sera sera, I believe. And hearing stories about how quintessential nice-guy Pete Friesen (the guy who invented the unified jacking system Expert House Movers uses in nearly all their work) has gotten the short end of many sticks in his 50 years in the business and STILL is a nice guy, it lets me know I'll be in good company when negotiations break down, my house falls into the ocean, and I pay taxes on this land till it's under water all the time. The story about the house being moved on trolley tracks and hitting the electrical line, which fell on the roof, burned the house, ignited the tractor's gas tank and, when it was unhooked, ran off down the street and plowed into a gas station makes me wonder, though, about how much last-place poignancy my biography can handle.

On a more positive note, "Keeper's" new owner called at 7:15 p.m. to say he's just fine — they went for a beach walk with a rescued greyhound this afternoon and "Keeper" behaved himself wonderfully on his leash. He's adapted to his new digs and seems contented. It's a great relief to know that "Keeper" loves living indoors with animal lovers — it doesn't really matter who or where. I know I was very special to him, but I'm relieved that that's not a one-person role. God bless that little guy, who'll always carry with him a piece of my heart.

The 1998 Keeper's House Move

In the first part of 1997, the fullness of Mary's life in New Hampshire, with her extended family of parents, siblings, nieces, and nephews, coincident with a brief lull in Keeper's House move planning with CCNS, meant that she didn't visit the Cape until May. With the completion of the Lighthouse relocation and her gift of the Oil House to NLPS (and its relocation), Mary's journal entries suggest a slightly new phase in her life as she began the 15th volume of her journaling with the following quote as prologue:

> We do not receive wisdom,
> we must discover it ourselves
> after a journey through the WILDERNESS
> which no one else can make for us,
> which no one can spare us, for our
> Wisdom is the point of view from which
> we come at last to regard the WORLD.
> — Marcel Proust

And in one of its first few entries by Mary, after a three- to four-month hiatus:

Monday, April 6, 1997: It's not that I don't need the outlet that journaling provides, it's that I need to value the effort and time necessary to "report in" more often from the mad map of loci I seem to end up in while following my curiously random Life Path. And so, I grab a few minutes out of a sun-drenched midday and, sitting in the pooled warmth and wind-break of my bedroom porch, here in New Hampshire, jot a few messages to myself.

The April fool's day blizzard leaves only scattered shoals of snow on the pallid lawn. The March-like wind seems to limber up the apple branches

177

which survived the weighty snow and howling winds of last Monday's storm. The sky is perfect blue with scattered wispy white streamers over the Dartmouth Ski-way. I've traded my morning garb for shorts and a T-shirt, and the heat of the sun on my milky skin feels positively therapeutic.

Mother's carpal tunnel surgery is scheduled for next Thursday, leaving me little leeway to put off a necessary trip to the Cape to see about repairing the garage roof, look at lots for sale (rumored) along Cable Rd., measure the distance between my septic pump-out and my well (!), check up on "Keeper" and his owner, meet with the folks at the Cape Cod National Seashore, give a story to Debbie S (journalist) on my plans to relocate the house elsewhere, and finally to transplant Miriam's broom plants, iris, and roses from the ocean side cliff edge.

I remind myself I am due for a mammogram tomorrow, which could tell me something far more consequential: the root cause of this year-old uneasiness in my shoulder and chest wall on the right side, including the nature of the "ridge" of tissue Dr. L felt in the dreaded mirror-image spot at 11:00 in the right breast. For weeks (until last week), I've been hounded by fears of recurrence, even at this late (?) date, of my breast cancer. I've thought how poignant that I counsel others in bearing up through breast cancer diagnoses, when I may be still in those woods myself. I've found myself praying that I not be asked to leave my life just yet — I've work to do, places to see, surrogate children to "raise." It sounds, in my own mind's ear, like "Please, Dad, I don't WANT to come home now. We're having too much fun..." which appeal always fell on deaf ears before, so I don't know why I think this might turn out any different. It's sad. And unnecessary. Why, am I not the one preaching to Mother about leaving bridges out there in the future to be crossed only when arrived at? Yes, I am. Well, then — practice what you preach, O Wise One...

Mother's Day, May 11, 1997: *...and I am far from where a dutiful daughter oughter B... Sitting at the Keeper's bedroom window, basking in rare morning sunshine, peering down some 80 feet to the polished skin of the Atlantic as it soothes the winter beach with its glistening foam. I can't* *yet see the high-water line, but almost — and each low tide since I arrived three days ago has displayed for me, in full prophetic view, the foundation ring from the last of the "Three Sisters."*

The warning is not lost on me... or on anyone else who gathered across the road last night for the ceremonial re-lighting of the relocated and restored Nauset Light. Before I went to bed, I stood out in the sandy circle where the Light was sited a mere six months ago and let the brilliant white and subdued red beams wash over me in the moonless cloudy air. Unlike in past years where that spot was directly underneath the protective beam sent out in a radial warning to floating structures approaching deadly shoals, now my Keeper's House (and I) were two of those warned structures. In just six weeks, the cliff edge has inched some 15-or-so feet closer to the Keeper's House foundation, till just 40 feet remains on the far side of it, and seven still-living evergreens stand like the last rank of a pine army, poised to sacrifice themselves to the enemy Gravity. The hydroseeded "lawn" is buried under an inch of blown sand. Only the 6 to 8 feet nearest oblivion is green, having survived the brutal excavation of last November's Lighthouse relocation. That fertile fringe is studded with Miriam's botanical bequeathal, iris, daffodils, rose bushes, yucca... though I've searched in vain for the Derby-Harry memorial broom plant, finding only a broken stump where I believe it used to be.

Downstairs, beneath each window and indoor storm panel, I found a small beach instead of a white sill — sand having seeped in on the sheer uninterrupted power of the nor'east wind, which picks it up from beach and cliff and hurls it at the house now bereft of its arboreal protection.

But this beach view is spectacular, even without the former stout red-and-white iron guardrail to visually hold on to. And I did sleep much much better last night with my "night light" back in service. No matter that it distributes itself in all-new patterns throughout the house, and that its brilliance is startling, like regular silent, intense lightning that fairly flames against these white walls. It is not the comforting soft gentle recurrent glow of last fall, now that we are in its beam, rather than beneath it.

Friday, I took my realtor's map and listings and drove about the ocean side of Eastham to see maybe 10 available half-acre to one-acre lots which are my alternatives to relocation and eventual capitulation to the Cape Cod National Seashore's reserved plot across the road next to the light... back under the beam again. But everywhere I went, I could hear Rte. 6 traffic instead of the ocean, and while the lots seemed nice enough for new construction, they were admittedly far <u>beneath</u> the standard of bearing a National Register-listed historical treasure like my Keeper's House. This house on any of those lots would look like a war orphan, a penniless emigre with no future prospects.

Jane and Ed's next-door situation is even more dire, however; in the April 1-3 nor'easter they lost 18 feet — virtually half their remaining front yard, and had to have their septic system pulled. There is not enough land remaining for them to even fit in another system, a well, and a foundation. The deep end-of-an-era/end-of-the-line depression this instilled was what kept them away from last night's relighting ceremony.

Friday night, I went out to dinner with International Chimney's Rick L, in town for the relighting, and to meet with the Nauset Light Site Supervisor and the Highland Light Site Supervisor. Over swordfish and oysters at the Lobster Pot in P-town, we agreed to pursue the latest official-though-skeletal rumblings from the CCNS Superintendent, that there is a better compensation offer forthcoming than her "last, best" offer of virtually no help at all, on 12/20/96. If we can come to agreement within the next three weeks, when ICC's contract with NLPS/CCNS will close, ICC will do my move to the site set to receive it, over next to Big Red and Li'l Oily. God, I hope we can do this. It's now MY number one priority.

Set forth on paper now are all the considerations that enter into this decision-making process: pros, cons, and to-be-resolved issues. There are so many variables in this equation, each linked, it seems, to a hundred unanswered questions. I regret having to go home today for (here I'll say it) mere Mother's Day — rather than staying to begin the hard work of resolving it all. Then again, perhaps it's best that I do as I was told and go home and await further instructions... while my realtor continues her now public search for alternative sites for me and my Keeper's House to move to.

From the Keeper's Log (same weekend), Mary added: *As I was preparing a "media packet" to hand out to inquiring reporters this past week, the Superintendent called to alert me that the CCNS offer of 12/20/96 may be superseded soon by a better one — one in which the Park either reimburses me for the cost to move across the street, or for the equity I have in the structure. So, although I would still be caught in their forfeiture trap, I would not lose absolutely everything in the process.*

The Light tower shines brilliantly even as a daymark, in its shiny new paint and crystal clear glazing. Even the over-clearing of pines at the south end of its reservation sets it off like a jewel on display — it simply never <u>ever</u> looked better. Even "Li'l Oily" fairly glows on its new foundation and with its new door (scavenged from Highland Light). All it needs now is a new cupola-replica to replace that lost in the awesome April Fool's Day Nor'easter. Our duty to history and posterity is 2/3 done. On with the final chapter so we can go back to measuring the erosion at the Light's new, almost confident remove.

8 June 1997 (Keeper's Log): *And the wondering continues — will the K.H. get lucky? Or wet?*

Evidently there has been no progress since 4 weeks ago — the Nauset Light Preservation Society and the National Seashore still aren't sure which will receive the federal $$ to save this place — so <u>no</u>body's driving this bus. I'm helping an appraiser do an appraisal of the worth of this structure, so I can evaluate anyone else's opinion and resolve this terminally interminable impasse. I think I've decided on a fallback lot a mile away, as the house rolls, but I hope I won't have to put any collateral where those unrevealed thoughts are. Meanwhile the ocean is showing little mercy — this week's unsettled nor'easter-like conditions tell us it's still so hungry it could eat a house. This morning, bright and early, following the nice reunion with the designer of my book, I set to work mowing the desert the movers left behind

— one 3-½-foot-tall rye grass stalk per two square feet — and (scary as it was) digging out a couple boxes of Miriam's gorgeous purple-blue iris from right at the edge of the cliff and all interwoven with poison ivy: double botanical jeopardy!! The pups have had their ocean swim (at Newcomb Hollow). I've had my annual Captain Linnell food fix, and tomorrow I'll head back home and continue to wait for the other side to demonstrate a talent for something other than brinkmanship.

At least old Mew (18 in August) benefited from this trip, outside all day and regaining her two-week-absent appetite for solid food. And I lost $110 — not at the Belmont racetrack at the Triple-Crown Challenge (which Silver Charm did not, alas, win) but 12 miles from Rte. 6's "Suicide Alley" section, to the Mass. State Police. I'm sure they'll make good use of it. Maybe it's time for me to either get a radar detector or slow down. Anyone want to wager on THAT?

"The Lightless Keeper" 6/8/97

P.S. Hoist a shot of hi-test to the 20-year-old Craftsman low-end lawn mower which still starts, each spring, with 10 pulls and a dram of WD-40 up its nose... Hip-Hip-Huzzah!!!

Sunday, June 22, 1997: *Since last visit, I and people around me seem to have drawn some more bonus cards in this life's game. The Cape Cod National Seashore says they now not only have money and the will to pay for the complete relocation of my Keeper's House, but they're willing to accept a donation of my remaining land, saving me from serving a sentence of paying taxes for life on a $300K piece of eroding real estate. This news, together with learning that Andy's research grant has been funded (after having been turned down 3 times last year), and that Mom has finally agreed to take a spot at Harvest Hill, together suggest a blessed shift of circumstances on all fronts, after a quite extended period of stasis. The period of constancy provided a fertile environment in which to practice faith and to recite — with more hope than resignation — "I'm not dead yet!"*

Unfortunately, and sadly, it was shortly after this that Mary found that the 17 years of ulcerative colitis she had most recently suffered through had turned into colorectal cancer. Her journaling of her Keeper's House experience during this time reflects a heightened sense of urgency, almost as if her very life was being captured in living metaphor by the pounding of the surf on the shores of her staunchly cherished but now all-too-tenuous home.

For the next few months, the latter half of 1997, Mary was fully occupied with treatment of the two tumors found in her colon, and did not have a chance to visit the Cape again until November.

Tuesday, November 4, 1997: Lois, a woman new to Lyme, whom I met as the next elder-to-me arrival on the Lyme Foundation Board, just called to ask me to be one of the Lyme authors who read from their original works monthly at the library. Sure, I said, ham that I yam, when? March it is, and I shall use that brash promise as a whip to get me to at least start doing the revised and updated version of "Nauset Light: A Personal History."

Maybe the first essay will be about knowing when to give in, let go, allow yourself the honor of knowing you have fought the good fight and — although you have not won — you have advanced the cause as close to winning as was humanly possible.

I gave my guts to save that Keeper's House and maybe that was unavoidable. Maybe it was too great a price to pay for "almost winning." And maybe who cares. At least it can serve as a musing-point for an essay for the second edition of my magnum opus-ette.

Tuesday, November 11, 1997: I recall, when I first got word that the two tumors I harbored were malignant, feeling that nothing had changed — I just now KNEW something I didn't know before. All else remained the same, and yet EVERYTHING WAS NOW VASTLY DIFFERENT and might never be as it was again. Once or twice, I caught myself laughing really hard at something and almost feeling the delicious nourishing, healing endorphin-release... And then across my path, only for an instant, like some overdone film effect, fell the shadow of the knowledge that what lay within me had the power to kill me, to turn all the lights out forever, to put an end to this amazing adventure that is my life, almost before I had really realized how to live it. I always stepped over that shadow, but I never forgot its chill.

Thursday, November 20, 1997: *New Hampshire's Roman Catholic Bishop O'Neill, who has been dealing with multiple myeloma for several years now, was recently hospitalized for fatigue and pneumonia. While there, it was discovered that he also now has leukemia, precluding further treatment for the bone cancer. He says when he heard this news, "a great peace came over me" and he asks us all for prayers for his strength to deal with his now doubly terminal condition. Gladly I will add him to my prayer list and marvel at his candor.*

<u>First</u>, *I will marvel at the "great peace" he says he felt when receiving a second death sentence — every time I feel a twinge in my right breast, up near my armpit, I experience a huge though brief sinking feeling. I'm sure that, now, were I to be informed of a recurrence of breast cancer after seven years of remission, it would not be "peace" I'd be feeling — it would be the world's, <u>my</u> world's, deepest inconsolable sorrow, borne by rage. I am a much smaller Christian than Father O'Neill. On his scale I am barely visible.*

<u>Second</u>, *I will marvel at his ability to encompass the contradictory (it seems to me) concepts of feeling this inner peace from God and wishing for outer support from mere mortals such as we. If one has the former, who needs the latter? I guess we all do. None of us is either all heaven-focused or worldly — until we leave this life, we are both. Bless Father O'Neill for reminding and inspiring me.*

God Calling[7] today says: "Know that Whatever the future may hold, it will hold more and more of Me. It cannot but be glad and full of joy. So, in Heaven, or on earth, wherever you may be, your way must be truly one of delight."

Thursday, 8 January 1998 (Keeper's Log): *On April 29th, I've consented to read to my townspeople from my writings about Nauset Light. Part of me says, "Let them buy the book and read it to themselves!" The rest of me (a smaller part) tries to appreciate the compliment and notices the impetus it provides to get to work and process last November (1996's) move of the Lighthouse. It's all here, in my journal — common ore with, one hopes, enough value-content to justify the energy it takes to refine it. These library readings have been wonderful, not only for their headlined readers (all more accomplished than I, really) but also for their power to attract interesting folks to one place at one time in a clear demonstration of what a unique, literate community I settled in, quite by chance. I'd best not disappoint or disillusion such nice people.*

Monday, March 30, 1998: *Today is the day they give Lighthouse Keeper's cottages away, returning them to their original owners. The United States Government, of, by, and for the people... Except that everyone but me and my friends will have to wait another 25 years to actually realize the benefit of setting foot in it. Will this distinction be fun to explain and enforce? I sure hope so, but I have my doubts. Perhaps I should invest in an enforcement implement. Perhaps an oar would be perfect — one of those 16-footers from a Hurricane Island pulling boat, set across the lap of the Daubenspeck serving perimeter enforcement duty from a lawn chair on the porch.*

This idle though amusing speculation is going on while all the participants in this extremely slow-moving saga call each other on the phone for info and reactions only to find the "phonees" have to go because they're waiting for other more critical calls from other "phoners." I myself am waiting bemusedly while the Superintendent waits for my lawyer to call her back so she can patch me in for a conference call about the quitclaim deed and Special Use Permit signings. Evidently a contractor has been chosen — though it's apparently not International Chimney, I understand, since someone in Falmouth submitted a bid of under $100,000. I'm not supposed to know any of the details, but I'm really disappointed in the outcome.

Working with Val would have allowed me a great deal of comfort and confidence that my needs and welfare were being considered at all turns. Now, I'll have to do battle with the contractors myself. (The medical costs resulting may push their actual costs over $100,000 — little do they know what dealing with me is like, especially on my home turf, albeit shifting...)

Monday, 30 March 1998 (Keeper's Log): *The Lightkeeper's Cottage at Nauset Light was placed in civilian foster care in 1955 when its last keeper was laid off and its parental overseers, the U.S. Coast Guard, had insufficient funds to care for it any longer. Today, professing solvency through swirling smoke and ever-shifting mirrors, the federal government has regained custody of this aging child, as, in a silent solo ceremony, I signed a quitclaim deed relinquishing my ownership forevermore. Never again will a mere private citizen motivated by love alone possess this small grey treasure.*

Just two such mortals, Miriam Rowell and myself, both childless women, enjoyed that fleeting pleasure and privilege, for just 43 years of the House's 123 years of service. The transference took place in too small a setting: I stood at the counter in the tiny insurance office that shares our Lyme Center, N.H., post office building. The insurance agent's wife stood ready with the notary stamp and we passed the deed across the counter for her secretary to sign as a witness. In two minutes the act was done. I made a small speech to supply context for the historic event, telling the two women their signatures were part of Lighthouse history now, but neither one was impressed. It was an unseasonably hot day and there was another customer to be waited on, a man insuring a '91 Chevy Blazer.

I came back to the house feeling as if I had squandered money. It felt like a beach day, despite the lingering presence of snowbanks along the wooded driveway sections, so I changed into shorts and a T-shirt and sat out on the deck in limbo for a couple of hours. If I closed my eyes, I could imagine myself on the front porch of the Keeper's House, 60 feet above the ocean, feeling the salt summer breeze and my sun-warmed face. Something we'd not be doing for another several decades, I thought, since following the relocation, the house will sit back in the woods next to the Lighthouse.

We'll have to be content to sit on our reconstructed patio and smell the Pines — or on the front porch with a whacking-oar across our laps to fend off the occasional errant misbehaving tourist.

I was going to have a gin and tonic but I fell asleep instead, awakening only to warm and eat a microwave-meal before calling it a day. As I drifted off to sleep, I composed an e-mail message to the National Seashore Superintendent. The quitclaim deed said, "In consideration of the sum of one and no/100 dollars..." but there was no dollar enclosed in the envelope it came in!

"Show me the money" the message would begin. But who was left to find any of it amusing? "The deed is literally done," I wrote the next morning, "but where's my dollar?" The message went unanswered, as I somehow expected. "Perhaps you're framing it for later presentation?"

Tuesday, October 4, 1998: *I am preparing myself and the pups to travel to Eastham tomorrow to begin overseeing the Keeper's House relocation project which is finally going to begin, with the pre-relo house survey. Six weeks from now, I should have a new lease on shoreline life (literally!) lasting me and my heirs 25 more years. (Although, I must admit the struggle took an enormous part of the joy out of "winning" this lifetime/25 yr. tenancy from the ostensibly hyperacquisitive Cape Cod National Seashore: a prize I have not yet officially been awarded.)*

Red/white stake marks former position of lighthouse prior to 1996 relocation. Less than 25 ft from Keeper's House to cliff edge at this point (October 1998).

As I am no longer the owner of the house (as of 3/31/98), and have not yet signed the Use & Occupancy Permit Agreement, I am not allowed to stay in the place during the relocation prep-work! Instead, after kicking and screaming about the eviction, I've been granted use of a Park employee cottage out behind Park headquarters, at $15 a night. That could amount to a lot of rent, but I'm beginning to think that this move might prove a lot less interesting to watch than the tower-move was. And with Mom still at Alice Peck Day for rehab from her re-pinned broken hip, I'll likely be on-site for just the middles of the six weeks of the work... and, of course for the actual road-crossing.

Larry, the U.S. Army Corps of Engineers supervisor of the project, has managed to get the well and septic system work added to the work order, at last, so it seems that in 6–8 weeks the place may not only be relocated, but also habitable. That would be nice: then I could go down and begin the unpacking of all the stuff moved up into the first floor areas from the basement and garage. It will take a few weeks of work to reclaim the living areas and restore them to cleanliness and tidiness again.

That will actually be welcome work — and through it I hope to recapture my love for the place, which has lain in a dusty corner of memory, wholly unuseful to me or anyone else since last October. One year of virtual aban-donment cannot do anything nice for an old house.

Wednesday, October 7, 1998: *The house-mover didn't show up for the pre-move survey. What does that tell the engineer and I, who <u>did</u>? Or are conclusions unnecessary? Probably. At this late date.*

No matter — in touring my presumably familiar house with this young engineer, I learned a whole lot more about it than perhaps all I thought I knew. I noted its notched 7" x 9" main beams in the cellar, its 5/4 beveled baseboards throughout, its one horsehair plaster wall and its widespread use of the earliest wallboard: vintage 1920s... skim coated with plaster so the painters weren't working over heavy brown paper!

Another more contemporary discovery was a refrigerator still full of condi-ments and formerly frozen food heading south fast, ever since the electricity was shut off 2 weeks ago! Tomorrow's tasty task is to clean the thing out — on a day when the dump is closed, wouldn't you know. I hate the thought of sharing auto space all the way to NH with those vintage noncomestibles, but I guess I see no alternative.

The second task is more pleasant, digging out Miriam's red climber rose from its recent home by the front steps — where to put it? I think I'll heal it in on the lee side of Jane C's new foundation, and hope it makes it through the winter. Then I'll gather a few more living-space essentials, like hangers and chair pillows, and finish making my own temporary quarters basically livable, out here behind the Park headquarters building.

This is a salvaged, transplanted (from Truro), refurbished "cottage colony" structure, as basic as these '40s–'50s cabins ever were — two 10 x 10 square bedrooms, an equally square 10 x 10 living room with a little kitchen and bath off it. Lucky for me, these five cottages have all just been rehabbed and they're as nice as they can be.

At about 6:45 I remembered there'd be a just-past-full Harvest Moon coming up out of the ocean sometime soon, so we drove over to the Keeper's House and sat in the dark awaiting it. I sat on the third step of the front porch, with the pups above and behind me, wondering why on earth we were out in the cold and dark like this and can we go home/in now? At times, in those admittedly uncomfortable 45 minutes, I had one cold nose/warm ear on my right shoulder and another on my left; I wish I had more than a mental picture of that.

When it seemed as if the show would never begin, we decided to drive down to the Seashore parking lot to wait out the rest of the cold preliminaries in our warm Explorer. But as soon as I saw the cloud furrows beginning to lighten above the horizon, we drove back to Our House and sat again on Our Steps to watch its birthing: it began like an orange campfire glow, blurred and amorphous, assuming roundness as it rose ever so slowly. A moon's diameter above the horizon sat a mask of black clouds, and as the orange orb passed behind it, it found a place where there were two openings I swear were eye-shaped, making the moon resemble a Hallowe'en mask set in the sky.

Back here in our little cottage, we feel displaced but cozy. I do believe sleeping in the darkened Keeper's House would have been a tad scary, even with my two ever-faithful guard dogs on my bed. I feel so far from Alice Peck Day Hospital — this is another, more real world, and I am delighted and blessed to be here.

Thursday, October 8, 1998: *Yesterday I brought from the Keeper's House one skillet, one saucepan, one paring knife, a can opener, 2 mugs, 2 Tupperware lidded containers to eat from, 2 spoons, a fork, and a knife. From Lyme I had brought a radio, a towel, a washcloth, dog sheets, pillows, my winter sleeping bag, my Army Corps of Engineers hard hat, and some clothes and other necessaries. I feel like Henry Thoreau. THIS IS WONDERFUL: to pare down and live simply, and Lord knows with my Lyme house now crammed with Mom & Dad's things as well as my own, it is the exact opposite of "pared down." Years ago the call of minimalism came to me from Colin Fletcher's book, "The Complete Walker," and I loved the planning and organization that went into outfitting a pack and a car for backpacking trips, whether just overnight to Valentine's woods or for six weeks in the American*

West/Northwest. I know I can do with next to nothing, and it is a luxury to do so.

The pups took me for a walk before dinner, a speedy one, as we expected the rain — long-awaited, all day — to materialize any second. Taking a long-cut through the Park's maintenance area (graveyard for not only beach metal debris but also culvert pipe, dry hydrants, granite blocks, telephone poles, concrete piers, and iron posts...), we set out along a "sand-line" trail through the woods — an extension of the one we used on this morning's relief run. Within about a mile and a half we were at the Atlantic White Cedar Swamp trailhead and the Marconi site.

The grey and lowering skies had turned the ocean an oil-green color and, try as I might, I couldn't make out Nauset's beacon. (Is it now too low? Or too forested?) One reason for taking the hike was to earn one of the lovely beers I had rescued from the Keeper's House refrigerator, which is now cleaned out, as is the garage of all that remained to be salvaged and (luckily) stored in Jane's new basement next door. The last task (aside from picking up shingle-pieces from all over the patch) was to transplant Miriam's red climbing rose once again, its second uprooting in a year and a half. I tucked it into a southwest-facing corner by their deck stairs, where it will get afternoon sun, some rain, and little wind. Miriam's can of rose food, vintage 1979, finally came in handy, though I had to coax the stuff to dissolve.

Wednesday, October 14, 1998 *(at Park cabin, Marconi, Wellfleet): Today was a memorable one. In it I acquired a car and lost a garage. I started off the day by signing a purchase agreement with Flanders & Patch Ford in Lebanon, to acquire a new Explorer replacement for my 1992 vehicle with 132,000 original (me) miles on it. It had taken me awhile to see the light, but this morning I bought it, and immediately drove it to Nauset Light.*

By the time I arrived at the Light, Gary's excavator was bashing its way through the Keeper's House garage roof, which made for a stunning photo opportunity. Before the rain set in, his crew had the shrubbery all removed and the garage hauled away, the basement cleared out and the foundation site across the street all cleared. Wow — this move is really happening!

I celebrated at Hearth 'n Kettle, having an Old Fashioned with my lunch/dinner — the day had seemed a week long. After catching up on my ledger and bills, I am ready for a full 8 hours of sleep, as east of me the surf sound carries 1-½ miles from Marconi Beach.

Thursday, October 15, 1998: Construction equipment hasn't always fascinated me, but today's experience of being near a piece with no one but its friendly owner-operator around was too good an opportunity to resist. Ask and it shall be given — and it was. I dug up a few shovelfuls of dirt by my former patio, fascinated with the fluidity of the two electronic/hydraulic "joysticks" that, with practice (says Gary), become extensions not just of your body but your *mind*. Ohh my! It was a rare treat, probably exchanged for my agreement in saying officially that, yes, I saw him excavate the old first cesspool in the pair supposedly buried thereabouts. To go rummaging in the trees for that alleged system would have been counterproductive and ecologically insensitive... besides the autumn olives that survived the lighthouse move wished to survive this one as well — and they deserve it.)

Wednesday, October 21, 1998 (at the Keeper's House relo site): An autumn breeze out of the northwest blows right through the basement of the Keeper's House, past nothing but the chimney base and exiting through the dozen or so beam-pocket holes that have been poked in the foundation walls. The excavator has about finished its work, carefully removing soil from under the now-hanging front porch without so much as nudging its structural supports. If there had been treasure buried on the site, I always thought it would be found under that porch, but he says he's found nothing but dirt. The street-side yard has lost its familiar terrace, and another autumn olive tree/bush its very life, but the damage is about done.

In touring the basement with Ernie and Frank of the Army Corps of Engineers this morning, I noticed the current foundation actually bows out (flares?) at the bottom, leading Ernie to believe it was poured atop the *footings as the house was perched in air above them... which is what they plan to do this time, as well. Sounds counterintuitive to me, but they claim it'll make for a perfect match of building to footer (even though the latter is poured with four inches of leeway on either side of the wall to play with.) We also noted the frost wall was poured separately from the foundation, and that's what gives the cellar floor that sill all around the edges. For historicity, we'll preserve that across the street, too.*

Pouring Keeper's House foundation at relocation site just southwest of Oil House.

Removal of one-car garage from Keeper's House prior to relocation.

Completion of Keeper's House garage removal.

Keeper's House is prepared for separation from its foundation.

Keeper's House loaded onto dollies, ready to move across street to new site.

. . .

Keeper's House pulled back away from original foundation, here seen moving up driveway across Nauset Light Beach Road to new location.

As seen through the Lighthouse port, the Keeper's House is moving up the driveway, but must navigate around the Oil House.

View from the Lighthouse tower of the Keeper's House moving up the drive to its new site (October 1998).

LightHouse and Oil House just prior to Keeper's House re-siting in the area to the right of the Lighthouse.

Keeper's House being cautiously navigated around Oil House en route to final placement.

Keeper's House being backed in past Oil House and Lighthouse to its final relocation point.

Keeper's House being gently guided to new foundation site.

Keeper's House is set on weight-bearing pallets at new site and moving dollies are removed.

Contractors making adjustments as Keeper's House is prepared for construction of new basement walls.

Keeper's House sited at new location, ready for finishing work (October 1998).

Monday, November 9, 1998: And this is the first chance I've had to write in this volume in an eventful 2 weeks, during which the Keeper's House was relocated across the street. It was a dream come true — a dream I've polished and rehearsed for 16 years, I guess, though when it happened I almost missed witnessing it, and after it was over, I couldn't believe it had really been accomplished.

The Friday before the move (it was October 23rd), the Superintendent's assistant at CCNS, emailed me to say that since the house wasn't jacked up yet by the end of the day it probably wouldn't move on Tuesday as planned, but on Wednesday instead.

Early Tuesday morning, I was bustling about my kitchen in Lyme, packing up to leave around 11, so as to arrive the afternoon <u>BEFORE</u> the actual move, so I could take some "before" photos of the support mechanisms... when the phone rang. It was the Superintendent's assistant saying the house was moving that very morning! ...and was I coming out? Although for some reason I was civil on the phone, I have never been angrier in decades than I was once I hung it up. I swore like a stevedore, causing both dogs to run for the door. Even the deaf cat left the kitchen. In 15 minutes I was ready to roll, and by 12:08 p.m. we were on the relo site, in time for the lunch break, with the house parked at the West side of the road, and the old foundation just a launchpad (cellar floor) and some crumbled gantries (the east wall's crumbled remains).

I had missed the scary gravity-fed trip down off the old foundation, with the fate of the structure riding on the brake pedal of Gary's tractor cab. But I saw that episode reprised when the house coasted ever so slowly over its new footings later that day. Having seen the end of the move (and the whole Lighthouse move two years ago), I can well imagine the part I missed. And Frank (Larry's fill-in) promised me duplicate prints of his pre-move and early-move photos from up close.

But it's the principle of the thing. All the way out to the Cape I thought, How many more ways are there for CCNS to show me the back of their hand? Frank assures me it was not malicious, but he agreed that it was incredibly thoughtless, and illustrative of how inconsiderate those folks can sometimes be when communicating with others...

But never mind... the important thing is that the house is safe for the next 75 years!! (one hopes).

There are hundreds of details, and some more battles to wage, before the house is rendered useful to me once again, but no hurricane — not even a Mitch-sized one — will claim her from that cliff edge, as might have been the case even yet this fall or winter had we not acted when we did.

Tuesday, November 10, 1998: *As I ended this entry, I was amazed at how inarticulate I had become. I wonder, is it tiredness, is it impatience and cynicism vis a vis the ultimate COMPLETE resolution of this relocation project and all its attendant problems? Is it boredom in working on this one equation for soooo many years? Is it the strange sadness I've noticed I harbor about this place which has never turned out to be the "joy nexus" I'd envisioned it could have become back in 1982?*

Something there is that keeps me from feeling again, or sustaining, the joy I did truly feel on the day the house was rescued two weeks ago. It's as if, through it all, I've been a hired hand — Miriam Rowell's agent — plotting and planning and agonizing over the rescue, and now I am feeling the post-game let-down. Do I want to continue to be the person who manages this place in its new public milieu? Do I welcome the inevitable dealings — good and bad — with the public, as both unpaid interpreter and tortured protector of my part of the Nauset Light Station?

Face it, I tell myself. It hasn't been the once-imagined joy. Instead, it's been a badly managed business/hobby, this maintenance of the place for others to enjoy, rhapsodize over, celebrate family milestones in. My own family has kind of taken it for granted from the start. Tim and his kids have been my most loyal sharers of the place, in summer anyway, and I fear that even they will soon grow beyond its recall. I fear that I am like my Keeper's House, old and charming and a lovely person/place to visit. How many times have I said I wish I knew a Mary Daubenspeck who would take care of this place and all its problems for me, so I could breeze in and out from

time to time, leaving money and house presents in my blissfully discon-
nected wake.

How did I get both feet so mired in this salvage project? Where might I
have planted them if not here? Surely, SOMEONE would have played my
part as rescuer at least *as well as I know I did. And if so, which face in the*
admiring transient crowd two weeks ago would have been mine?

This afternoon, just an hour or two before the much-needed rain arrived,
the pups and I high-tailed it out onto our white woods-path to the
Marconi station site. This time we added the Atlantic White Cedar Swamp
Trail onto our itinerary and so covered about two miles, all told. From the
cliff edge, the beach as far as the eye could see was deserted, as the light
green ocean laved the smooth, endless beach with small, white-fringed
waves. That everlasting vista felt renewing to me and, as always, perspec-
tive-restoring.

Now, after a quick frigid swim and dinner, the pups are curled up on the
couch in our cozy little "Vaclav Hovel" (my name for these temporary Park
Service quarters generously supplied for me), where we'll spend the night,
then head back north to winter tomorrow morning.

This was not an essential trip, by any manner of means, but it was impor-
tant and I wouldn't have missed it. Tomorrow is Veteran's Day. I can
honestly say I feel like one.

Relocation Aftermath and Mary's Final Battle

Thursday, December 17, 1998: In the interview yesterday with the editor of ORION magazine, the phrase was born:

> The absurd spectacle of mere mortals
> Disputing temporal title to a parcel
> Of shoreline which has always been,
> Is now and evermore shalt be – Being
> Reclaimed – yea, verily, devoured:
> Eaten up and spat out elsewhere –
> By cosmic geologic processes anyway...

This is the object of all of Life's experiences — some personal perspective on the Whole of It. And it is painfully long in coming.

15 August 1999 (Keeper's Log): *The intense few weeks' work to reopen this house and restore it to its former hominess — ostensibly in time for Gillian and Chris's wedding which was to have been held here August 5th — was good therapy during and after the loss to all of us of Gillian's mom, my brother's wife, and my dear friend Sarah Freney (9/30/39–8/6/99, far too few years). The committal of some of her ashes to the ocean she had so hoped to return to was as moving an experience as the final week-long vigil by her bedside. And the Pleiadean meteorite that arced its way across our sky as we stood on that darkened shoreline underlined what we know to be painfully, painfully true — that everything we have — including those we love beyond words' telling — is but lent to us for a time. This relocated treasure of a house is an emblem of survivorship — I hope my brother Andrew will find when he comes here, a way of returning to himself as well as to the site where we four stood and said another sad goodbye to the love and light of his yet-young life.*

I am so happy to be back here in this living room after twenty-two months of being locked out! I can't say I love the changes outside this front door, but at night, when I can hear the sound of the surf now a comfortable distance away, I drift off to sleep imagining it a closed chapter in a book with a lot more pages in it...

Mary Daubenspeck

(no longer an owner, now a mere "user and occupier," but happy to be here nonetheless...)

26 August 1999 (Keeper's Log): *Yesterday at National Seashore Headquarters, in a spectacularly ordinary and under-attended meeting with the Superintendent, I signed the 25-year "Use and Occupancy Permit" for the Nauset Light Keeper's House... and somewhere a federal clock began ticking away our tenure here. Although the relocation is still depressingly incomplete (viz. the peripheral moonscapes surrounding the leaky foundation, the multiple missing downspouts and screens, the bounty of scrap piles within and without the cellar, the overland phone line often mistaken for a fallen clothesline), and the guilty parties are nowhere to be found. INSIDE, the place seems like home again. And in these past four vacation days, delightfully shared with brother Tim, along with Ben and Heather, I find that my initial delight (circa 1982–3) in having such a remarkable second home has come flooding back. The calming sounds of the ocean are comfortably distant once more, and although the front yard's new public status is difficult to get used to (mostly due to lack of signs — something we are told is correctable perhaps within our lifetime), coming home to it at night is a recovered joy and the warmth of the lights its windows cast at the foot of the only-slightly-dimmer beams of "Big Red" are as welcoming as once they were, when I gave little thought to the future of this handsome trio of historical treasures. All's well that ends even reasonably well, I say, and hoist a gin and tonic to the memories of this house these volumes contain, the old and new friendships they document, and all that is yet to be written within them. It's the very beginning of a distant end, and I for one am ready to enjoy it.*

— Mary

1 December 1999 (Keeper's Log): *Clipper and Polly and I are down just to put up the storm windows, inspect the new patio, itemize the contractor's omissions, appreciate the "lawn," test the new two-zone (upstairs, downstairs) heating set-up, and attend a very official meeting at Park Headquarters: something they are calling the Annual Performance Review. At this new adversarial get together they will tell me what I should do differently, with my dollars, around here; and then they will seek an accounting from me of where all the millions of dollars in rent I must be pocketing each year here are going. I've compiled an Income vs. Expenses balance sheet (P&L statement) for 1982 to 1999 which shows that only in 1984 did the place make money — some $400.00. In every other year, it's run a $4000–$15,000 deficit. I think their profit-placement worries are a tad extreme. They'll also want to know what sort of one-sided shrubbery I plan to surround the new patio with — so that the branches won't extend beyond 18,000 feet from the house and into THEIR AIRSPACE.*

Ah, but that's tomorrow. Today in the 50-knot gusts, I'll sit and listen to the house flex and breathe as it always did, the comfortingly slow tick-tick-tick of Miriam Rowell's plastic kitchen clock marking our time, and I'll rerun in my mind's theater the spectacular site we saw at sunset here and at Coast Guard Beach — a pink sky above a broad lavender horizon, a steely blue-gray ocean rising in 10–12 foot waves cresting in white foam... and, above it all, gulls washed pink by the sunset's light soaring and standing still in the whipping winds. It was nearly too much to appreciate all at once and without the camera.

Mary's next (and last) full year (2000) was fraught, with the insidious loss of her health to the recurrence of her colon cancer, during which time she had limited ability to visit her beloved and now relocated Keeper's House. Although she suffered greatly during this time physically, her deep love for her family and her abiding Christian faith enabled her to strike a spiritual balance that (mostly) fended off depression and allowed her to make the most of the precious time she had remaining. At one point, describing a July evening in 2000, she wrote in her journal, *"We went to the co-op and I bought steaks and salads and cheeses and dips, and we brought Mom up and all of us — Tim, Andy, me, and Mom — all had a celebratory 4th of July dinner on Andy's wonderful screened porch overlooking the valley and Mt. Ascutney, with the sounds of a foggy summer evening wafting all about our lively conversations. I believe I could live for a long, long time if I can stay tightly bonded to my truly enviably wonderful family."*

Excerpts from her last few entries in the Keeper's Log reflect something of her grasp of the importance of the success of the recent Keeper's House move, her devolving health, and her love of family, all being felt in some form in virtually every moment.

In July 2000: *It is a dream come true — and perhaps just in time. I'm on the first of two weeks' vacation from the chemotherapy which has done little in the past 5 weeks to give us a lot of confidence. So, we'll try the new "killer agent," starting on the 18th, after the family reunion in Harrisburg, PA. It almost killed me in April, in combination with the standard two agents I've relied on for the past 5 weeks. But as a solo treatment, I hope hope hope it will give me many more months to enjoy my beautiful Lincolnville Wherry, now readily available to me in that lovely, protected cove in South Orleans. (Thanks to my friend Mimi's generosity, allowing it to be moored there this summer.)*

In August 2000: *Just a week after enjoying nearly 7 days here with Andy and his grandkids, et al., I have returned with another brother and his delightful entourage: Tim, Ben, and friends — and I have spent the past three days defying the totally erroneous weather forecast that nearly kept us from coming down here... summer days at Nauset are a balm for the soul, a timeless constant in my ragged-edged life... I'll be back again, God willin', late next week when baby brother Steve and his fambly are here. This new way of regarding this place — as a family clubhouse — is so refreshing, compared to the seemingly endless view I used to have, since about 1986, of the whole thing left to topple off the cliff and into the ocean whose surf-sounds everyone ELSE could wax rhapsodic about, as I saw only their advancement ever closer to my basement! This is truly a* *wonderful refuge which I hope to enjoy, in all seasons, for the rest of my life. And sharing it is such a joy*

— Mary

In October 2000: *October 14th was the day we hauled my boat out of Horseshoe Cove in South Orleans and took her home to New Hampshire for the winter (because there was no storage space locally and because it will be easier to do her fitting out next spring up there where the tools are). It was a whirlwind trip, down and back the same day, with biggest brother Joe and big brother Andy — both of whom performed heroic service in the hauling, and, the next day back in my Lyme driveway, removing what constituted a 16-foot aquarium exhibit from the "Kestrel's" planked keel: algae, seaweed, sponge-that-resembled-tan-coral, great mops of seagrasses, even barnacles and little crabs — all had to be evicted with snow-scrapers, vinegar, and a high-powered hose. She'll need her bottom repainted next spring, but the summer harbor dwelling was worth it, just to see her in her element, gently swinging on a mooring line, outshining her neighboring vessels in the summer sunshine. Aren't we all happiest when we're where we feel we were always intended to be?*

And her final entry, **11 November 2000 (Keeper's Log):** *This place has become, once again, such a wonderful "old shoe," now that it has been relocated to safety and re-outfitted somewhat for human habitation. Of course, it still could use a new dishwasher, garbage disposal unit, and a couple of twin bed box-spring/mattress sets, but it is once again a joy to be able to come down here for a few days with family and/or friends. Seeing it anew each time through the eyes of others is always a treat — no one fails to be touched by the same effect it seems to have on newcomers, just as it had on me almost exactly 19 years ago when I first visited Miriam Rowell here to scout out the place for possible purchase. Seems like only yesterday...*

As the end drew near for Mary, in early 2001, she was able to make her last wishes known. One of those wishes was that I, with Andy's help, would assume management of Keeper's House operations for

209

the remaining 23-year term of the CCNS lease. I agreed without a moment's hesitation.

Mary died on March 24, 2001, at Dartmouth-Hitchcock Hospital in Hanover.

A Service of Thanksgiving
for the Life of

Mary Eleanor Daubenspeck

June 21, 1944 · March 24, 2001

Flexible, beachable, more open to
Altered course, mind, destiny.

MARY E. DAUBENSPECK LYME, NH — *Mary E. Daubenspeck, 56, died Saturday, March 24, 2001 surrounded and supported by family and friends. Having survived two types of cancer, a recurrence of a third proved insuperable. To the last, she was buoyed by the unfailing support of her five brothers and her mother, and still strove, as a Bryn Mawr College English major, to leaven life among her overwhelmingly engineering-oriented family. Having wished for a medical career, studying pre-medical subjects in college, Mary concluded that perhaps her wish was too unspecific, for the medical career she got cast her as a patient rather than physician. Born in Denver, Colo., Mary grew up in Stratford, Conn. and spent much of her adult life in the Philadelphia, Pa. area before building her dream house in Lyme Center, N.H. in 1991. Her greatest joys in life were her brothers, who added eleven delightful and talented nieces and nephews to her childless life. She counted among her treasures, her strong faith and her many* *friends, not to mention her lifetime collection of boats and antique wheeled vehicles. A staunch protector of her 1982 acquisition, the 1875 Keeper's House at Nauset Light Beach, Eastham, Cape Cod, she saw it through a protracted and contentious relocation by the National Park Service, safely now 300 feet from the ever-eroding cliff and the relentless ocean. She shared this historic structure and its dauntless spirit with friends and relatives, and its history with everyone, through her 1995 book, "Nauset Light: A Personal History." She also edited the recently published "We Had Each Other: A Spoken History of Lyme, New Hampshire." An enthusiastic and inquisitive freelance writer and editor, she wrote frequently for Dartmouth's graduate school publications, deriving great pleasure from making complex subjects entertaining to ordinary folk like herself. For 30 years, Mary was her college class notes editor, linking 315 people she counted as friends. She also donated her writing and editing skills to many civic and nonprofit organizations, including the Upper Valley Humane Society and the Lyme Historians. She served as a director of several organizations, including UVHS and the Lyme Foundation. She served as past president of a thriving theatre just outside Philadelphia, where she lived and worked before relocating to N.H. She was also a graduate of the first all-women's 26-day Outward Bound course at Hurricane Island, Maine. Mary is survived by her mother, Eleanor M. Daubenspeck, of Harvest Hill, Lebanon, N.H.; and by five brothers, Josef B. Daubenspeck of Marysville, Pa; J. Andrew Daubenspeck of Lebanon, N.H.; Timothy H. Daubenspeck of Colchester, Vt.; Peter B. Daubenspeck of Harrisburg, Pa.; and Stephen M. Daubenspeck of Harleysville, Pa. She is also survived by eleven nieces and nephews; four grand-nieces and -nephews; and by her loyal, faithful, and attentive mother-daughter Labrador Retrievers, Clipper and Polly; and her adopted stray cat, Toby White. Together they grounded her independent life in simplicity and love, and taught Mary in the last months the rare and precious art of living in the present. A celebration of Mary's life will be held at St. Thomas Episcopal Church, Hanover, N.H., on Saturday, April 7, 2001, at 3:00 p.m. with a gathering of family and friends at the Lyme Academy Building in Lyme Center, N.H., to follow. Burial will be in Highland Cemetery, Lyme, at the family's convenience. In lieu of flowers, memorial contributions may be sent to any of the following: Upper Valley Humane Society, Enfield, N.H.; the Lyme Foundation, Lyme, N.H.; or the Class of 1966 Mary E. Daubenspeck Memorial Fund, c/o Bryn Mawr College, Bryn Mawr, Pa. Arrangements are under the direction of the Rand-Wilson Funeral Home of Hanover, N.H.*

Wishing to spare her family the anguish of composition under duress, and partly because she knew that none of us would (or could) write it as well as she could, Mary penned this, her own obituary. Her proficiency and love of writing enabled her to reflect broadly on her life and create something measured and meaningful, and at the same time quite beautiful — as evidenced by the many comments received by the family after it had been read in the newspapers.

In the epilogue to Mary's final authored article, *One More Byline*[6] (Dartmouth Medicine Publication), Andy contributed the following eulogistic insight:

Epilogue: *Mary Daubenspeck died a month after her last journal entry — on March 24, 2001. Her brother Andy says, "Mary's last days were difficult. She never gave in, really, to the idea that she was dying. Her mind accepted palliative care, but her heart never did. She struggled to the end, which was very hard for those of us who loved her — we wanted her to suffer less than her struggle permitted.*

"Since Mary's death, her beloved Keeper's Cottage has become a focal point for our sense of loss (even, sometimes, anger); we spend time there doing things we used to do with her. Mary felt a special sense of stewardship for the Keeper's Cottage. Situated next to the Nauset Lighthouse, it symbolized for Mary part of the connection of humans to something bigger, something beyond the concept of 'owning.'

"In the same way, Mary was and still is her family's lighthouse. Her family and extended circle of friends are aware that Mary continues to inhabit our thoughts and feelings, affect our course, light our way."

Family Use of Keeper's House 2001–2024

Mary's passing, and the invocation of the CCNS Special Use Permit (SUP) signaled a new era of Keeper's House operation within our family. By this time, Mary had acquired a brood of nieces and nephews who had become thriving children and teens possessed of the good fortune to have visited the Keeper's House for vacations in virtually every year of their relatively young lives, to the point at which it had become instilled in our collective psyche as an important part of what we all do. The 25-year CCNS permit, although significantly more restrictive in its terms than private ownership had been, did effectively guarantee our family the opportunity to regularly enjoy time at this most spectacular and hallowed Cape place by the sea — that is, of course, with the mutual understanding that we continue to maintain and preserve it as the valued historic structure now listed in the National Register of Historic Places (per M. Rowell and Mary).

With a limited amount of funding Mary had bequeathed to help us in picking up the Keeper's House management reins, Andy and I immediately spent a goodly portion of it on a sorely needed new roof. Because the Special Use Permit (SUP) prohibited for-profit rental, and because Andy and I both had full time jobs and family responsibilities off-Cape, it was imperative for us to establish a set of effective operational guiding principles for long-term use and sustainability.

We agreed that the house would be used, maintained, and preserved with the support of a collaborative of family and close Keeper's-House-loving friends, such that every visitor would be either a family member or well known by one or both of us — and that the house would be used exclusively as the quiet "family" place Mary had always intended it be. Thus has every Keeper's House visitor been not only very familiar but has understood that they will treat the House as if it were their own during their stay, taking responsibility for managing minor issues, replacing key staple items, and thoroughly cleaning it prior to departure with a "leave-no-trace" theme — and an additional objective to leave it, if possible, cleaner than found at the beginning of their visit. At the same time, we've fostered and encouraged direct and open communication with each guest, through which it has been possible to address routine maintenance issues in real-time as they have arisen, without any apprehension or anxiety on the part of the visitor. In this way, the Keeper's House has always been occupied by caring, responsible people who've loved and appreciated it for its cozy comfort as well as for its natural and historic attributes.

Further, Andy and I shared the deep conviction that the interior décor and layout configuration of the house ought to be preserved in original configuration as a memorial to Mary, who had set it up in the understated but elegant manner that lends comfort and grace to the basic rustic character of the Lighthouse Keeper's quarters. There was no need to make any significant change — it was already "perfect" and the way we felt it should be. Our job was to keep it so. This was a driving principle of our effort, extending even to the "GO AWAY" cocoa mats (inspired by Mary's sense of humor), that confronted potential guests and visitors at the stoop of both primary entry doors.

Keeper's House kitchen, northwest view.

Keeper's House kitchen/dining area, full view.

Keeper's House master bedroom, east (ocean side) and south wall view.

Keeper's House library/living room east (ocean side) wall.

Keeper's House window seat area, south side.

Classic nautical bar area.

West wide of sitting room and chart wall.

First morning sunlight streaming onto master bedroom west wall.

View out front door to the ocean.

As with any vintage 1875 house, though, the Keeper's House is by nature in a state of gradual continual deterioration, and long-term preservation requires much more than just frequent cleaning. Over the years (since 2002) we've replaced the roof, re-shingled the south, west and north sides, fully replaced all five of the large first-floor windows (two south, two north, one east), the large south-facing basement window, and the north-facing master bedroom window. We've replaced the north and south basement-level exterior doors with solid, well-made air-tight ones. We've installed a water pump activation switch to prevent possible absentee basement flooding issues, performed structural reinforcement and repair to the north-facing front porch on several occasions, and have replaced the hot water heater, clothes washer, gas dryer, dishwasher, and gas stove/oven range. Exterior trim and interior wall, ceiling, and trim maintenance have regularly given rise to an often-significant painting line item in the annual budget. The first- and second-floor bathrooms have each been renovated once during this time, with a new shower, corner flooring, and privy on the second floor, and new flooring, lighting, and privy on the first. These preservation activities together with routine maintenance of fundamental systems, the comfortable interior, weathered exterior, and grounds, have placed aggressive regular annual demands on our budget, invariably consuming all available funds and more — the annual deficits replenished faithfully by family.

Routine management responsibilities for such a place do not come devoid of challenge, and the Keeper's House is no exception. The seaside location is an intensifying factor, with regular high wind and foul weather concerns. Maintaining a year-round, round-the-clock vigil from 325 miles away can be trying at times. Frequent off-season storms, interior system or appliance failures, errant burglar alarms in the middle of the night, maintenance projects with contractors, etc., have often conspired to necessitate unplanned spontaneous trips to address, correct, or supervise. It has not been unusual to warrant nine to ten trips during the year from Vermont to the Keeper's House— typically for several days at a time and always with a work objective as primary, but usually (although not always) with an attendant opportunity to experience some quality time as well. "Keeping" the Keeper's House is indeed a labor of love though it can test one's mettle at times, as it almost daily requires some attention.

And yet, it has worked. Family and friends have built their vacation plans regularly around time at the Keeper's House while finding with children and grandchildren, nieces, nephews, and adult siblings and partners a wealth of joy, solace, and respite.

Keeper's House Regulars. Four Daubenspeck Brothers, (L–R, Tim, Andy, Steve, and Pete) in Keeper's House kitchen, March 2024. (Beloved eldest brother Josef B Daubenspeck passed away in 2021.)

With gladdened heart and resolve, the Daubenspeck brothers together have embraced this rare opportunity to both preserve the house as a valued historic treasure and an important "touchstone" to Mary and to enable many other beloved family members and close friends to enjoy the understated elegance and prime summer vacation location of the Keeper's House in similar manner with their families. In response, the Keeper's House itself has thrived. It is not a stretch to say that the House is in better shape today than it was in 2001, just by virtue of it having received more constant and continuous domestic attention per year than it had during the disruptive few years of relocation and Mary's illness.

In 2021, during a status presentation to the Cape Cod National Seashore, the Superintendent at the time commented that our stewardship of the Keeper's House has been exemplary, and that we have, by virtue of our caretaking performance, set a "high bar" for others to follow, referring to our efforts as having virtually inspired an effective "gold standard" for Park properties.

Now in 2024, the National Park Service will take over a fully functional, current, very accommodating, and remarkably comfortable house — an honorable tribute to Mary's passion and tenacity on its behalf — and to Miriam's, Mary's, and the Daubenspeck family's private stewardship over the past cumulative term of 65-ish years.

In her first book,[3] Mary describes some of the attributes that make a lighthouse so appealing to so many of us — its illusion of permanence, abundant strength, certainty, constancy, and reassurance. Add to that the spiritual symbolism of a beacon of light cutting through fog and darkness. It is a romantic and compelling image that universally pleases and inspires the heart. A great poet might have said, "Nothing there is that doesn't love a lighthouse."[8,9]

But what is it that makes the Lightkeeper's House so alluring — and so vitally satisfying a place to be for family and friends? Some idea about this can be surmised from a few of the Keeper's Log testimonial excerpts left by family and friends over the years.

November 8, 2001. A brief visit indeed in chilly but sunny weather... didn't know how I'd feel coming here the first time since Mary's demise — thought perhaps we'd just be sad — but her spirit prevails in the serenity of this space, and while I was putting "our" garden to bed for the winter I began to feel she hadn't gone far after all...MB

October 4, 2003. The house is quiet now and feels comfortable and secure, the only sound the ticking of the clock and the wind outside. Mary's Keeper's House is a real grounding point for the soul. From here, I often have a strong sense of the "external" nature of all that is chaos and worldly confusion, and an awareness of a peace that lies within — and ultimately unaffected by all that...TH

July 16, 2005. I alternate between feeling a stranger and feeling like a distant relative while here. I devour your history and your Keeper's journals like a hungry student, and I am caught up in your magic and love of this place and all it means to you as a family. I love the legacy of this home I have come to know. I want my home to radiate the same love and warmth...DA

October 1, 2005. There are places, shared with others, that always seem like coming home. The play of light on walls, shadows of rotating red, the soothing sound of night waves. Glorious fall days of crisp dawn, rosy along the rolling horizon, sun and breeze all sparkle by day. No one on the beach this morning as the sun rose, then a few fishermen and surfers...SC

October 3, 2006. Brilliant, sunny day — perfect for cleaning windows this morning. How much easier it is to clean when it feels like you are caressing a memory, and doing your part to keep light coming into this special place. In the picture of Mary in the master bedroom I notice her hands and how strong and well used they look. As I do my small part here, I think of her touch now, and although it's not necessarily the right thing to say, with such a fine, strong grip it must have been very hard for her to let go. How clever she was to appoint you all as such loving caretakers of her lighthouse legacy...ES

October 10, 2006. In returning to this magical place, the loss of the love of my life became more painful. There were constant reminders of his vitality — gaiety — childlike wonder — love. Through these soul-clouded days, I want to tell you that the sun is breaking through, and renewing my spirit... As the Nauset Light beams become his steady beacon, flashing 3-second messages of love and gratitude, it tells all who see it of my love for a life-saving spouse... AG

October 14, 2006. Something magical about this place. All cares seem to lift and, for a brief moment, life is full of nothing but joy and peace. In every season and every light — one of my favorite places in the world...ET

December 23, 2007. I can feel the history and the memories here. Wind and sea teach us of the ephemeral, transitory nature of all that is now. But a thread runs through this place that is a true privilege to share. Thank you, Tim and family. Thank you, Keeper's Cottage...BD

October 5, 2008. I knew Mary only briefly in her last few years, as a soft spoken, gentle spirit whose goal in life was clearly to save this dwelling from the long-armed reach of the ever-encroaching sea — to bear witness to one person's steadfast dream is to glimpse both faith and courage in a tangible and meaningful way...MG

October 18, 2008. The stock market has tanked, the economy is treacherous, the national mood has become somewhat desperate, yet this place still serves as an unfailing refuge here at the foot of the Light. I'm reasonably sure the world won't come flying apart, but if it did, I would come here, where things are free and easy and where there is always to be found strength and sustenance for the soul and spirit...TD

September 1, 2012. I feel like every time I come here, I become more and more part of a collective of people and experiences that honor the history of the Lighthouse, the legacy of the family, and specifically, Mary. Each trip I linger a bit longer gazing at the revolving light, I meander a bit more through the house looking at the photos, the artwork, running my finger along the spines of books on the shelves, pausing here and there at interesting titles. The sounds of the old floorboards flexing are a comfort as familiar as the soft sound of the crickets at night and the soothing lull of the ocean. It is a privilege to honor the Lighthouse, the family, and Mary, and I am truly humbled...MK

In April 2015, the Keeper's House was used by special arrangement for the filming of four scenes for the movie *Year by the Sea*, based on the book by Joan Anderson, and featuring actresses Karen Allen and Celia Imrie. The director related that Karen and Celia enjoyed the warm comfort of the Keeper's House during the day (Monday, April

27, 2015) while resting between the four scenes. Karen and Celia signed the Keeper's Log as follows:

— "Dear Tim, We loved visiting your beautiful Lighthouse. I'm sure it will be a beloved scene in the film *Year by the Sea*. Thank you for sharing it with us. Best, Karen Allen"

— "Thank you, Tim. What a way to spend a Monday morning. So exhilarating — Unforgettable... I want your 'Go Away' mat — may I please? With love, Celia Imrie"

June 21, 2019. What a magical place. My parents have spoken of the Keeper's House with such fondness for years, this summer we finally got to join them. I get it. The sense of character and history here is tremendous, a window into another era, tended with love. Cold and foggy for our visit, we have nevertheless been struck by the haunting beauty and romance of this place. The lighthouse standing vigil outside our window, gold-white beam stabbing through the thick fog, will forever be etched into memory. I will treasure these memories forever. Thank you to those who've kept this place and this legacy...JP

October 27, 2021. As I write this, there are 70 to 80 mph buffeting winds and rain pelting the house from the northeast. The used-to-be line between air, sea, and land has been obliterated by the storm that started yesterday night. The power and water are off. There is no sign of the Atlantic from any window, though we can hear it roar. The work on the Lighthouse has left her dark, which adds to our sense of singular isolation. And, really, that's what we came here for. I'm not surprised to find how sturdy this house is in a storm. You feel her quake and list, responding to the wind, but she stands her temporary ground... The house was pristine upon arrival. I love seeing how with each visitor, the Keeper's House stands up straight, flattens her shoulders, and welcomes us in. With all of her visitors she becomes more rich and comfortable. What a gift you Daubenspecks have given to us — Mary most of all. Blessed to be here...BS

September 17, 2022. There are certain experiences in life that we take in on a sensory level. This place is one, a house surrounded by unbelievable beauty and grace. You might expect that sleeping within feet of a huge, strobing, searching light would keep you awake. Ironically, NO! In fact, I had the deepest most peaceful sleep I've had in years! The Lighthouse keeping us safe... Thank you, Tim it was unforgettable...AE

Tim and Mary Daubenspeck, ca. 1995.

A Lasting Keeper's House Legacy

Thus, Mary and Miriam's many years of private ownership and shared vision now culminate in Mary's living landmark legacy, with an impact cast in multiple dimensions. To the general public, to Eastham, to Cape Cod, the successful effort by Mary together with the Cape Cod National Seashore and the Nauset Light Preservation Society to re-link the Keeper's House to the Lighthouse and Nauset Light Station permanently, is without a doubt the legacy aspect that benefits the greatest number of people. Eastham, Cape Cod, and the Cape Cod Potato Chips company retain their emblematic identifying icon in a physical site presence that can be easily visited and generally appreciated for its historical significance as well as for its natural beauty.

Perhaps the deeper and more penetrating legacy, though, is the one that befits Mary's family and friends. For we who've had the privilege of an ongoing personal experience of the Keeper's House for the benefit of not only ourselves but our families, our children, and grandchildren — the untold enrichment of together-time over the years has fertilized raptured hearts with indelible memories and grown us each ever a bit closer to one another — against the backdrop of what seems at times to be an outside world torn asunder.

Our wearied human soul needs a place in which to be able to truly relax in physical and spiritual comfort, with the awareness that no matter what may be going on externally, there can be sustained a quiet sense of peace and order within. The Keeper's House "Keeping" mission entered my own life unexpectedly at a time of inner unrest and great spiritual tension, in which personal loss, single parenting, and relationship and career commitment posed challenges on every front. My Keeper's House "calling," though emergent from a moment of acute sadness and loss with Mary's passing in 2001, has, over the years, proven to have been a gift unforeseen, affording me the exceptionally rare and fulfilling privilege of loving and caring for this revered "nexus" of family interconnection and jeweled living metaphor of strength in the face of unpredictable adversity.

To open the door to the Keeper's House on a visit to the Cape has been to escape to another world of space and time, with permission to leave the routines of life and the world behind and become genuinely "present" in its simply appointed yet elegant, stately, welcoming, and gracious space — space that feels at once familiar and safe. A place in which one might experience a vibrant and memorable celebration of family and friendship in one case, or find a haven of sanctuary in introspective solitude in another, depending upon the particular circumstance. At the same time, Mary's spirit is to be found everywhere within its walls for those of us who knew and loved her, fostering a lingering feeling of accessibility — a thread now ever the more difficult to release.

To have had unfettered access to Mary's inspired, hallowed, and historic house suffused with so much character and personality has been a blessing incomparable for all of us these last many years. That which has been given us here in the form of life, love, and family has become eternally ingrained within — and what has been written in heart and soul can never be taken away. Mary herself often said, "Everything we have is but lent to us for a time," but for our family and friend Keeper's House experience — that time has become everlasting.

Among other things, the Keeper's House has for most all of us, at various times, served as:

- a point of reunion and celebration of family together through the years
- a wellspring of spiritual renewal, solace and respite
- an easy starting point for a morning beach walk and a breezy lunch destination thereafter

- an inspiration for romance, engagement, and the vision of planning a life together
- a haven for quiet, reading, and meditation — with no TV
- an ocean idyll where surf is heard 'round the clock
- an oasis of creative energy for the artistic and musical
- a peaceful sanctuary imbued with a slowing of time and the lifting of worldly pressure
- a place to grieve, to remember, and to offer ashes in prayer to the ocean
- a lively lounge where cards are dealt, games are played, glasses are lifted at happy hour, and friends and family, kids and grandkids laugh and play together
- a steamy and abundant kitchen for "lobster night"
- an accommodating and gracious front porch for sunrise, coffee and breakfast
- a refuge at which to observe wildlife, birds of the air and sea, foxes, turkeys, bunnies
- a reassuring shelter of strength as it strains and creaks and braces against a gale force wind
- a warm and cozy nook — a comforting, safe (and almost irresistible) napping spot
- a personal lived experience of the Lighthouse site, with service to the House as an interim "Keeper"
- an extraordinary moment to feel its character and to connect with its 150-year history
- an unexpected adventure when huddling by lantern light during a blizzard of horizontal snow when the power is out
- a nurturing seaside retreat at which to reacquaint with innermost self and be blessed in spirit and soul
- a place to experience pure love without worldly distraction

As the de facto arbiter of the ultimate fate of the Keeper's House (and Oil House), Mary had multiple options at her disposal. From the standpoint of long-term financial integrity, a move of the Keeper's

House to a private lot in Eastham for the sole benefit of Mary and her family would have made great practical sense. The house and lot together would be easily worth several million dollars today. But it was her personal integrity that mattered more. Her choice against the financially viable option in favor of what in her heart she believed to be the morally appropriate one fulfilled her personal conviction and inspired a permanent legacy.

And so it will continue to be celebrated now in its sole public role as a correctly sited and permanent historic symbol of Eastham and Cape Cod — now once and for all time, "a tower **with** a setting and a setting **with** a tower."

For all of this we are eternally grateful to you, dear Mary...

Epilogue

Time often moves in a swift current, dancing, murmuring, each moment an eddy within a larger ripple of sense and sensibility in which the heart is a guide and our conscience a rudder. A noble course set and held steadfast in challenging seas can have profound and lasting beneficial consequences. Mary's enlightened view that we are only here for a time, that everything we have is but lent to us, and that in life we each have a personal responsibility to something that is greater than merely ourselves — along with her passion and commitment — have together inspired a principled and timely resolution of this "cliffhanger" of a tale, with the reinstatement of the Nauset Light Keeper's House and Oil House to their historic public status and the full reunification of the Nauset Light Station for the remainder of time.

At the same time, Mary's thoughtful and loving decision-making fostered a growing and lasting closeness among her family of Daubenspecks, an ever-to-be-cherished annual vacation experience, and the gift of stewardship of her beautiful historic Keeper's House — in the maintenance and preservation of which we may now take pride, as we hand over something that is at least as good as it has ever been — if not better. It was indeed ours for a time — a good time — and we were proud and competent stewards. And now it will be for everyone to enjoy.

Sunrise over the thin ribbon of land (barely 20 ft wide in places) that remains on the far side of the road where the Nauset Light station previously stood.

The thin ribbon of land that remains across the road where the Nauset Light Station once stood is now only about 20 feet wide in places (2024) a faster-than-hoped erosion rate signaling the possibility of another relocation — perhaps in the next 10 to 15 years. Whatever the plan specifics may be at that time, they will doubtless include and protect the three revered structures together in their authentic configuration, by virtue of the legacy of Mary Daubenspeck and her personal mission, as originally envisioned and inspired by her kindred friendship with Miriam Rowell.

A Keeper's House billow of clouds at sunset.

Acknowledgment

The smooth operation of the Keeper's House over the past 23 years would not have been possible without the support of the Cape Cod National Seashore, specifically in the person of Park Historian Bill Burke, the CCNS appointee for interactions regarding the Keeper's House. Bill has been as steady, conscientious, and committed a resource as one could hope to have. Through circumstances which have been at times challenging he has always been responsive and professional, upholding the highest traditions of CCNS while adding intelligence and pragmatism to address and resolve issues of consequence as they arose. As the face of CCNS to our family during the term of the Special Use Permit, Bill has personified all of the virtues of the Park Service, and his participation in the Keeper's House preservation endeavor is hereby most gratefully acknowledged.

Also, the support of Glenn, Keeper's House neighbor, friend, and Nauset Light Preservation Society member, is acknowledged with gratitude. In addition to being the Keeper's House Painter, Glenn has responded promptly on multiple occasions to perform house-checks immediately after storms and to help correct some of the unexpected mundane (but potentially critical) situations that occasionally have arisen over the years.

Finally, an acknowledgement of appreciation to Susan Abbott and the NLPS Keeper's House Committee for helping to ensure that the final transition of management responsibility in April 2024 was accomplished with clear and open communication and in a manner that minimized disruption for both parties — while consistently maintaining the Keeper's House itself as the foremost priority.

Oil House in first light of dawn.

Dusk view of Nauset Light and Keeper's House.

Bibliography

1. Chaucer, Geoffrey. *The Canterbury Tales of Geoffrey Chaucer: a New Modern English Prose Translation by R. M. Lumiansky, Together with the Original Middle English Text of The General Prologue and The Nun's Priest's Tale.* New York: Simon and Schuster, 1948.
2. Daubenspeck van Roden, Mary. *Nauset Light: A Personal History.* Black Rabbit Press, 1995.
3. Nauset Light Preservation Society Website, www.nausetlight.org
4. Thoreau, H. D. *Cape Cod.* Boston and New York: Houghton Mifflin Company, 1914. [PDF] Retrieved from the Library of Congress, https://www.loc.gov/item/14014155/.
5. Baillie, John. *A Diary of Private Prayer.* Charles Scribner's Sons, 1949.
6. Daubenspeck, Mary. "One More Byline." *Dartmouth Medicine* Vol. 29 No. 1 (Fall 2004). (https://dartmed.dartmouth.edu/fall04/html/one_more_byline.shtml)
7. Russell, A. J. *God Calling.* Arthur James Publishing, 1981.
8. Oblique reference to language style used by Robert Frost in Mending Wall.
9. Frost, Robert. "Mending Wall." *North of Boston.* New York. H. Holt, 1915.

Appendix

The Resident "Keepers" of Nauset
Light Keeper's House (1875-2024)

Occupant	Position / Term
Nathan Gil	Lightkeeper / 1875 to 1883
Stephen S. Lewis	Lightkeeper / 1883 to 1914
Thomas J. Kelley	Lightkeeper / 1914 to 1918
James Yates	Lightkeeper / 1918 to 1919
George I. Herbolt/John E. Poyner	Lightkeeper / 1919 to 1932
Allison G. Haskins	Lightkeeper / 1932 to 1938
Fred S. Vidler	Lightkeeper / 1938 to 1942
Eugene L. Coleman	Lightkeeper / 1942 to 1952
Miriam Rowell (Lucien)	Private Owner/Occupant / 1956 to 1982
Mary Daubenspeck	Private Owner/Occupant / 1982 to 1999
Mary Daubenspeck Family	CCNS Permittees / 1999 to 2024

www.ingramcontent.com/pod-product-compliance
Lightning Source LLC
Chambersburg PA
CBHW051142120626
46547CB00012B/909